M

and

My Salvation

My Rock
and
My Salvation

Meditations on Forgiveness,
God's Providence,
and the Christian Life.

by

Clarence J. VanderVelde

INHERITANCE PUBLICATIONS
NEERLANDIA, ALBERTA, CANADA
PELLA, IOWA, U.S.A.

Library and Archives Canada Cataloguing in Publication

VanderVelde, Clarence J., 1964-
  My rock and my salvation : meditations on forgiveness, God's
providence, and the Christian life / by Clarence J. VanderVelde.

  ISBN 978-0-921100-80-5

  1. Forgiveness—Religious aspects—Christianity. 2. Providence and
government of God—Christianity—Meditations. 3. Christian life—
Meditations. 4. Reformed Church—Prayers and devotions. I. Title.
BS491.5.V356 2008 242 C2008-901176-7

Library of Congress Cataloging-in-Publication Data

VanderVelde, Clarence J., 1964-
  My rock and my salvation : meditations on forgiveness, God's
providence, and the Christian life / by Clarence J. VanderVelde.
      p. cm.
  ISBN 978-0-921100-80-5 (pbk.)
  1. Bible—Meditations. I. Title.
BS491.5.V36 2008
242'.5—dc22

                                                    2007015153

Cover Picture *Mount Shuksan* by Clarence J. VanderVelde

Published simultaneously in U.S.A. by Inheritance Publications
Box 366, Pella, Iowa 50219

Available in Australia from Inheritance Publications
Box 1122, Kelmscott, W.A. 6111 Tel. & Fax (089) 390 4940

Printed in Canada

Contents

Preface

The title for this book comes from the opening verses of Psalm 62, which are also the subject of a meditation. Only when we confess that God is our rock and our salvation do we have peace.

The meditations are grouped into three topics which have been recurring themes in my ministry: forgiveness, God's providence, and the Christian life. I have found that these are the matters with which many of God's people struggle. Six of these meditations have appeared earlier in *Clarion: The Canadian Reformed Magazine* and are published here with permission.

I would like to thank my wife Theresa and my sister Margaret for proof-reading all the meditations and offering useful suggestions for improvement. Scripture quotations are taken from the New International Version, 1984 edition. Quotations from the Genevan Psalms, hymns, the ecumenical creeds, the Reformed confessions, and the Reformed liturgical forms are taken from the *Book of Praise: Anglo-Genevan Psalter* (Winnipeg, Manitoba: Premier Printing Ltd, 1993).

I hope that in these meditations I have spoken to both the head and the heart.

Clarence J. VanderVelde
Fenwick, Ontario
January 2006

Read: Genesis 3; Revelation 6:9-17

The LORD Clothes His Children After the Fall into Sin

The LORD God made garments of skin for Adam and his wife and clothed them.

Genesis 3:21

Everything narrated in the Bible serves a purpose in God's revelation of salvation. Sometimes we wonder why some parts of the Bible are so detailed and other parts are so brief, but it all has a purpose in the LORD's overall revelation of the gospel. The first chapters of Genesis are very compact, and we would love to know more about the things narrated in these opening chapters of the Bible. Precisely because these crucial events at the beginning of the world are narrated so concisely, we must take careful note of what is revealed. As far as Genesis 3:21 is concerned, we easily read over this text without realizing that these words are full of good news!

The LORD created man to live in fellowship with Him, but then the Fall into sin broke this fellowship. The first awareness that Adam and Eve had of the Fall was that they realized their nakedness (3:7). The man and his wife noticed their sinfulness at the core of their relationship because sexuality goes to the core of the marital relationship, and sin went to the core of all relationships. Sin results in feeling vulnerable and exposed, and nakedness exemplifies this. After the Fall, nakedness points to embarassment and shame because there is something to hide. Adam and Eve had such feelings toward each other and, therefore, they made coverings for themselves (3:7).

Then they heard God coming, and they hid (3:8). God was coming for fellowship with His children, but Adam and Eve knew that they had broken this fellowship by deserting to the side of the devil. Because they deserved and feared punishment, and felt exposed before the Lord, they hid from the Lord. But the Lord called out, "Where are you?" (3:9), not because He did not know where they were but because He was seeking them in His love and grace. The Lord went after His fallen children and was going to clothe them.

Underpinning the text is Genesis 3:15, with its promise of a Saviour, One who would crush the head of the serpent. God was going to continue His relationship with man, as is evident also from the still valid mandate to fill the earth with people and to develop the earth to God's glory (Gen 1:28; 3:16-19). This good news became very tangible in the fact that the Lord God made garments of skin for Adam and his wife. The very act of the Lord God clothing His children after the Fall into sin encapsulated the gospel of salvation!

Adam and Eve, however, were already clothed when the Lord made garments of skin for them. After the man and the woman realized that they were naked, ". . . they sewed fig leaves together and made coverings for themselves" (3:7). Were they clothed inadequately? Probably, because God made *garments* of skin for them, but Adam and Eve had made *coverings* of fig leaves. The Hebrew word for *garments* is used elsewhere in the Old Testament for the robes that people wore. Scripture teaches that God encourages modesty in our physical appearance.

More important, however, is the symbolic significance of the Lord's act. Adam and Eve tried to hide behind their clothing and thus were also engaging in a symbolic *cover-up*. Yet, when the Lord came for fellowship, they fled because they felt exposed especially toward God. Adam answered God's call with the words, "I heard You in the garden, and I was afraid because I was naked; so I hid" (3:10). Adam was wearing fig leaves but still considered himself naked before the Lord! Adam knew that God could see through the fig leaves and that their sin was in naked view before God. "Nothing in all creation is hidden from God's sight. Everything is uncovered and laid bare before the eyes of Him to whom we must give account" (Heb 4:13).

Then the Lord God made garments of skin and clothed Adam and his wife. Garments of *skin*! This meant that an animal or two had to be killed to provide God's children with clothing. These were the first animals killed in the history of the world. Blood flowed to provide man with clothing, and this blood pointed to the redemption through Christ's blood. The message right after the Fall into sin was that man can only live by the shedding of blood.

The symbolic significance of the Lord clothing Adam and Eve is borne out by Scripture's repeated mention of clothing within the context of salvation. Isaiah says, "I delight greatly in the Lord; my soul rejoices in my God. For He has clothed me with garments of salvation and arrayed me in a robe of righteousness . . ." (Is 61:10). In the Revelation, John sees the saints under the altar receiving a white robe because they are the redeemed (Rev 6:11). Therefore, the significance of the Lord clothing his children after the Fall into sin is that our sin is covered in the blood of Christ!

At the beginning of this fallen world, Adam and Eve ran when they heard the Lord coming. At the end, people will also be running when they see Christ coming in glory because they will feel naked and exposed before God (Rev 6:15-17). But between the running away from God at the beginning and the end of this fallen world lies the gospel. By God's grace, there are people walking with God — people whose sins are covered because they are wearing the garments of salvation.

Read: Psalm 86

God is Forgiving and Good

*You are forgiving and good, O Lord, abounding in
love to all who call to You.*

Psalm 86:5

We do not know the exact circumstances in which David
wrote this Psalm but we do know that David was having a hard
time because ruthless men were seeking his life (86:14). As a
child of God, David lifted up his soul to the LORD in prayer,
seeking his help from the LORD, as so many of God's children
do also today.

There is an important structural point about this Psalm
which we should notice because it adds depth to the words of
the text. In each of the first four verses the same little Hebrew
word appears, namely, a word which is translated "for" or
"because." Verse 1: "Hear, O LORD, and answer me, *for* I am
poor and needy." Verse 2: "Guard my life, *for* I am devoted to
You." Verse 3: "Have mercy on me, O Lord, *for* I call to You all
day long." Verse 4: "Bring joy to Your servant, *for* to You, O
Lord, I lift up my soul." Notice that in each of these verses the
word "for" appears in the middle of the verse after a specific
request. Then we come to verse 5 and that very same little word
appears again, but this time at the beginning of the verse. The
text says literally: "*For* You are forgiving and good, O Lord,
abounding in love to all who call to You."

This is significant because it means that verse 5 gives the
culminating reason for David's request for the LORD's help. In
each of the verses, David gives a reason for requesting the LORD's
help, but in verse 5 David gives the main reason. Verse 5 ties
everything together. In this, David goes from the lesser to the
greater. He begins by giving reasons which focus on himself:
for I am poor and needy; for I am devoted to You; for I call to

You all day long; for to You I lift up my soul. And then David gives the reason which focusses on God Himself: "For You are forgiving and good, O Lord, abounding in love to all who call to You." In other words, foundational to David's request for help from God is the character of God Himself! God is forgiving and good, abounding in love. David's boldness in asking for God's help is based on the forgiveness of sins. The forgiveness of sins is the basis for everything else in our lives!

David says that God is "forgiving and good." David realized that regardless of whatever else he may have experienced in his life, sin was his greatest misery. Of himself, David could not appear in God's presence because he was guilty and condemnable in the sight of God. Daily his debt increased with the LORD because he was conceived and born in sin and inclined to all manner of evil. David was aware of his sins and shortcomings. Therefore, who was David to ask for the LORD's help, as he does in the first four verses?! But David could ask because God is forgiving and good! There was reconciliation between David and God because God was paving the way to the promised Saviour who would pay the penalty for David's sin. By means of the Word of promise as well as the sacrifices and other ceremonies of the law, the whole Old Testament dispensation pointed forward to the coming of Jesus Christ (Heidelberg Catechism, Lord's Day 6 Q&A 19). Consequently, David knew that the LORD would listen to his prayer, for the LORD is forgiving and good.

David also says that God is "abounding in love." A very special Hebrew word is used which is very difficult to translate precisely. Different translations render it as "love," "steadfast love," "lovingkindness," and "mercy." All of these shades of meaning are part of this word. It is a word which conveys that God's heart goes out to His people!

David was bold enough to call upon the LORD because he knew that the LORD is forgiving and good, abounding in love "to all who call to [Him]." Yes, to all who call to Him . . . Calling upon the LORD is an act of faith, and the LORD loves those who come to Him in faith. David expressed his faith in various ways throughout this Psalm. In verse 2, he says: ". . . for I am devoted to You." In the verses 8-10, David says that among the gods there is none like the LORD; He alone is God. And in verse 11, David says: ". . . give me an undivided heart, that I may fear Your Name." With a heart of faith, David called to the LORD and knew that he had access to the throne of mercy by grace through faith.

As believers living in the time after Christ's accomplished redeeming work on the cross, we may be comforted and emboldened by the fact that we have a High Priest in heaven who is interceding for us. "Let us then approach the throne of grace with confidence, so that we may receive mercy and find grace to help us in our time of need" (Heb 4:16).

Read: Psalm 130

My Soul Waits for the Lord

My soul waits for the Lord more than watchmen wait for the morning, more than watchmen wait for the morning.

Psalm 130:6

In Old Testament times, watchmen stood on the city walls during the night to guard the city against attack. They were on the lookout for any danger that might lurk in the shadows of the night and threaten the well-being of the city. Not surprisingly, these watchmen eagerly awaited the arrival of morning because the night could be filled with danger.

When the Psalmist says that he waits for the Lord more than watchmen wait for the morning, he uses an image to which every Israelite could relate. We do not know the author of this Psalm, nor do we know at what time in Israel's history he wrote. We do know that he was in distress, because he begins by saying: "Out of the depths I cry to You, O LORD; O Lord, hear my voice. Let Your ears be attentive to my cry for mercy" (130:1, 2). Perhaps he was experiencing personal hardships that made him cry out to the LORD. Perhaps he was simply distressed by the reality of sin in his life, because he writes about sin and forgiveness (130:3, 4) and ends his Psalm by referring to redemption from sin for all of Israel (130:8).

Whatever the situation may have been, the Psalmist invokes an image of intense waiting. Waiting for the Lord occupied his mind and consumed his being. The Psalmist's frequent reference to waiting emphasizes the point. In verse 5, he says it twice: "I wait for the LORD, my soul waits . . ." In verse 6, he says it again and then underlines the intensity of his waiting with the image of the watchman, an image which he repeats twice.

What about us? Do we wait for the LORD with a sense of expectation? Perhaps we are passing through the darkness of personal difficulties or the night of sorrow and are waiting for the joy of a new morrow (cf. Ps. 30:3, *Book of Praise*). Are we waiting for the LORD to help us? Even more importantly, do we long for deliverance from this fallen and broken world with all its sin?

Notice the confidence which the Psalmist expresses in his waiting. He clings to his covenant God. Although he does not do so in the text, elsewhere in this Psalm the author uses God's covenant Name. In verse 1 he says, ". . . I cry to You, *O LORD* . . . ," in verse 5 he says, "I wait for *the LORD* . . . ," and in verse 7 he says, "O Israel, put your hope in *the LORD* . . ." The Name "LORD" — or Yahweh in the original — is God's covenant Name and points to God's love, grace, and faithfulness toward His people. The LORD has spoken words of promise to His people, and the Psalmist's waiting is characterized by hope in the LORD's word (130:5). In fact, the Psalmist says that ". . . with the LORD is *unfailing love* . . ." (130:7), and in saying this he uses a word which is often associated with the LORD's covenant faithfulness. All this makes the Psalmist exclaim: "O Israel, put your hope in the LORD . . ." (130:7). He urges the same confidence upon all God's people! Also us!

Yes, there is full redemption with the LORD (130:7). Ultimately this means that "He Himself will redeem Israel from all their sins" (130:8). The Old Testament believers were waiting for the promised Saviour who would obtain deliverance from the reality of sin as well as from all the effects of the Fall into sin. We call it the history of *redemption*. When Zechariah prophesied at the occasion of his son John's birth, he prophesied about the soon-to-be-born Christ and said: "Praise be to the Lord, the God of Israel, because He has come and has redeemed His people" (Lk 1:68). Of Simeon we read that "He was waiting for the consolation of Israel . . ." (Lk 2:25), and when he saw the Christ-child at the temple he said to the LORD: " . . . my eyes have seen Your salvation . . ." (Lk 2:30). Anna too was waiting, and when she saw the baby Jesus ". . . she gave thanks to God and spoke about the child to all who were looking forward to the redemption of Jerusalem" (Lk 2:38). Christ the Saviour was born to redeem us by His death and resurrection.

Again, what about us today? Waiting for the LORD means embracing His covenant promises with confidence. He will provide help in time of need so that we have the strength to bear distress. Even more importantly, He will deliver us from this fallen and broken world, and we have the hope of total redemption from sin and misery. We may await a new earth. The basis for our redemption was laid at Christ's first coming, and the full enjoyment of that redemption will be manifested at Christ's second coming. Within the context of writing about the brokenness of life in this fallen world, the Apostle Paul says that we ". . . groan inwardly as we *wait eagerly* for our adoption as sons, the *redemption* of our bodies. For in this *hope* we were saved" (Rom 8:23, 24). Waiting eagerly for redemption with hope — that is what Psalm 130 is about. We know more clearly what it means, and so our waiting should be that much more intense. The final and full redemption is coming!

Read: Matthew 7:24-27

Build on the Rock!

*"Therefore everyone who hears these words of Mine
and puts them into practice is like a wise man who
built his house on the rock."*

Matthew 7:24

The foundation of a house is crucial to how the house will stand up under the test of time. A house built on a foundation of solid rock will withstand a severe rainstorm, while a house built on sand will collapse as the sand shifts. A wise man gives careful thought to the foundation under his house.

This is the analogy which the Lord Jesus Christ uses with regard to how we construct our lives. The wise person is the one who puts Christ's words into practice and thus builds on the rock. Christ spoke this parable at the end of the Sermon on the Mount. His disciples had gathered around him, the crowd stood within easy earshot, and Christ delivered the sermon which has become so well-known. At the end of it all, Christ says that the one who hears these words and puts them into practice is a wise man.

The implication of Christ's concluding statement is that the wise man lives by faith in Him. Putting Christ's words into practice is a matter of living by faith in Him. Only someone who truly believes in Christ will live according to the words Christ spoke in the Sermon on the Mount.

The purpose of all of Christ's preaching was to show that He is the promised Saviour sent by God to fulfil all obedience for us and to pay the price for our disobedience. Christ even said in this sermon: " 'Do not think that I have come to abolish the Law or the Prophets; I have not come to abolish them but to fulfil them'" (Mt 5:17). By His holy living Christ did what we should have done, and by His death on the cross Christ suffered what we should have suffered. Here was the Saviour sent from above. His preaching was a call to believe this gospel and to build one's life on this gospel.

It is not enough to say that we believe in Christ, because we must also demonstrate this in our lives. Our faith must be evident from our works. "Not everyone who says to Me, 'Lord, Lord,' will enter the kingdom of heaven, but only he who does the will of My Father who is in heaven" (Mt 7:21). To mention but a few things: living out of Christ means being merciful (Mt 5:7), being pure in heart (Mt 5:8), and being peacemakers (Mt 5:9). It means not storing up treasures on earth but in heaven (Mt 6:19, 20), and it means not worrying about food and clothing but trusting that God will provide (Mt 6:25-34). All of this is an expression of our faith in Christ.

When we build our lives on Jesus Christ, we are like the wise man who built his house on the rock. Doing so leads to temporal blessings. Unless our lives are deeply rooted in Christ, the disappointments of life in this fallen and broken world can easily upset us to the point of total collapse. All kinds of storms of life can whip us, and only the person whose life is founded upon Jesus Christ as Saviour will have the defences to weather those storms. Otherwise there will be nothing to hold us up and keep us going.

More importantly, building our lives on Jesus Christ leads to eternal blessings. Then we do not have to fear the fierce torrent of God's anger against sin, because we rest secure in Christ. We do not have to fear these words of Christ on the day of His return: ". . . I never knew you. Away from Me, you evildoers" (Mt 7:23)! Then our eternal well-being is secure. One day the believer will exchange this earthly home for the eternal home.

Read: Mark 16:1-8

And Peter

*"But go, tell His disciples and Peter, 'He is going
ahead of you into Galilee. There you will see Him, just
as He told you.' "*

Mark 16:7

A few words, spoken almost as if in passing, can have great meaning. So it is with this text. The angel told the women who had found the tomb empty on the day of Christ's resurrection that Christ had risen from the dead. Then the angel said: "But go, tell His disciples and Peter, 'He is going ahead of you into Galilee. There you will see Him, just as He told you.' " What may seem as if spoken in passing, and what we may easily read over without much thought, is that the angel said: "Go, tell His disciples *and Peter* . . ." These words have great meaning. Of the four gospels, Mark is the only one which includes this detail. And, in the Bible, details are always important.

Peter always had been a leader and spokesman among the twelve disciples. When Christ asked His disciples who they thought He was, Peter was the one who made the confession, "You are the Christ, the Son of the living God" (Mt 16:16). Peter always had been an impulsive and brave man as well. When Christ explained to His disciples that He would suffer many things in Jerusalem, be killed, and raised to life on the third day, Peter took Christ aside and rebuked Him, "Never, Lord! This shall never happen to You" (Mt 16:22). Moreover, when Christ told His disciples after the institution of the Lord's Supper that they would all fall away, Peter declared, "Even if all fall away, I will not" (Mk 14:29). When the soldiers came to arrest Jesus in the Garden of Gethsemane, Peter was the one who took his sword and hacked off the ear of one of the arresting party (Jn 18:10).

That was how Peter was: a bold and brash man, a leader among the disciples, someone not easily unsettled.

Did the angel make special mention of Peter because he deserved special recognition due to His prominent position among the disciples? Not at all.

For, what had happened shortly after Christ's arrest? After Peter had boldly declared that he would never fall away, he denied his Lord the very same night! While it was bad enough that all the disciples had deserted Christ after His arrest in Gethsemane (Mt 26:56), Peter fell to the deeper low of actually denying Christ verbally: "I don't know this man . . ." (Mk 14:71). When the rooster crowed, Peter remembered that Christ had foretold his denial. One of the gospels even says that when the rooster crowed, Christ looked straight at Peter, and Peter remembered (Lk 22:61). That glance cut into Peter's heart. And then Peter went outside and wept bitterly (Lk 22:62).

We can well imagine that Peter's sorrow did not disappear instantly. The sadness about his sinful actions undoubtedly lingered in Peter's heart during the three days that Christ was in the grave.

And, therefore, already in the early hours of the day of Christ's resurrection, God had a message for Peter! The message would come to Peter by means of the women to whom the angel spoke. "Go, tell His disciples *and Peter* . . ." The women would undoubtedly say to Peter: "The angel even mentioned your name specifically!" That would be very moving for Peter, and he would know instantly the implicit message: God still wanted him within the circle of disciples! God would not cast him away because of his deep fall. Peter had fallen hard, but God still counted him in! Peter also had to go to Galilee with the other disciples. In this way, God comforted and encouraged Peter in the sorrow over his sin.

The significance of the words "and Peter" is that they encapsulate the gospel of the forgiveness of sins! God had seen Peter's broken heart and his tears, and God received him in grace. His sin was forgiven. And the messenger from heaven — the word "angel" literally means "messenger" — could convey this in these few words. Christ had died on the cross also for this sin of Peter. The angel proclaimed the gospel of forgiveness in these few words!

This has been revealed to us for our comfort. We are sinners. Daily we have to contend with the weakness of our faith and with the evil desires of our flesh. Sometimes we fall hard and are so very disappointed in ourselves. But when there is sorrow over sin and a desire to fight our unbelief and disobedience, we may be assured that God will not cast us away. God counts us in, just as He counted Peter in!

Christ Jesus Came into the World to Save Sinners!

Here is a trustworthy saying that deserves full acceptance: Christ Jesus came into the world to save sinners — of whom I am the worst.

I Timothy 1:15

Are we impressed with the gospel of salvation? Or have we become accustomed to it and take it for granted? The Apostle Paul was awed and amazed by the fact that Christ Jesus came into the world to save sinners. We hear his amazement when he writes, "Even though I was once a blasphemer and a persecutor and a violent man, I was shown mercy . . ." (1:13). And Paul elaborates on it when he says, "Here is a trustworthy saying that deserves full acceptance: Christ Jesus came into the world to save sinners — of whom I am the worst."

For people with a Jewish background — as Timothy had — the term "sinners" was a loaded one. In the gospels we find that it was used in Christ's day for those considered to be the vilest of people (e.g. Mt 9:10, 11). The self-righteous Jewish leaders classified *others* as "sinners," but Paul does not use the term in this way. Paul classifies everyone under this category because he writes that "We also know that law is made not for the righteous but for lawbreakers and rebels . . ." (I Tim 1:9). There is no one who is righteous (Rom 3:10, 11). And Paul includes himself in the category of sinners as the worst of sinners. This was not just a self-effacing humble statement. Paul meant it!

What had Paul done? Paul describes himself as once having been ". . . a blasphemer and a persecutor and a violent man . . ." (1:13). Paul had persecuted the church of God intensely in order to destroy it (Gal 1:13). The Book of Acts shows us Paul giving approval to Stephen's murder and dragging Christians off to prison during the subsequent persecution (Acts 8:1, 3). In all this, Paul had blasphemed the Name of Jesus Christ. As the Heidelberg Catechism explains, ". . . no sin is greater or provokes God's wrath more than the blaspheming of His Name" (Lord's Day 36 Q&A 100). Paul offers no excuses but openly confesses the depth of his sin and misery.

We too are sinners, albeit in different ways. Do we still have an awareness of our sin and misery? Do we realize that we are worthy of eternal condemnation as lawbreakers and rebels?

The amazing truth of the gospel is that Christ Jesus came into the world to save sinners! Paul emphasizes the comfort of this glorious gospel by saying that his deliverance serves as an example for those who would believe in times to come. As the worst of sinners, Paul says: "But for that very reason I was shown mercy so that in me, the worst of sinners, Christ Jesus might display His unlimited patience as an example for those who would believe on Him and receive eternal life" (1:16). Paul's deliverance holds out hope for us!

Sometimes believers do consider their sins, are even burdened by them, and ask: "How can God really want me? Is there really room for me?" Then we may take heart and remind ourselves that the mercy shown to Paul is also shown to us.

And then we can exclaim joyfully with the Apostle Paul: "Now to the King eternal, immortal, invisible, the only God, be honor and glory for ever and ever. Amen" (1:17). This is an expression of deep thankfulness. We have received a glorious gospel because it reveals to us Jesus Christ as the Saviour of sinners.

Marvel at the wonder of God's mercy!

God Wants All Men to be Saved

*. . . [God our Savior] wants all men to be saved and
to come to a knowledge of the truth.*

I Timothy 2:4

For Reformed believers, this passage often raises questions. There is no getting around the fact that Paul speaks about praying for all men (2:1), that Paul writes about God wanting all men to be saved (2:4), and that Paul says that Christ Jesus gave Himself as a ransom for all men (2:6). But don't we confess in the Canons of Dort that the Bible teaches the doctrine of limited atonement? Didn't Christ say, "I am the good shepherd; I know my sheep and my sheep know Me . . . and I lay down My life for the sheep" (Jn 10:14, 15)? And don't we confess in the Canons of Dort that the Bible teaches the doctrine of election? Didn't Christ pray to the Father, "I am not praying for the world, but for those You have given Me, for they are Yours" (Jn 17:9)?

The original Greek gives us an important clue to understanding the text. When the Greek language wants to present a definite number, it uses a definite article, but that little word is not used here. In Greek, this means that not the *number* is in view, but the *kind*. Therefore, Paul's statement about God wanting *all* men to be saved should be understood to mean that God wants *all kinds* of men to be saved.

This is supported by further evidence in the passage because Paul identifies one kind of people: kings and all those in authority (2:2). Immediately after saying that prayers should be made for all men, Paul mentions authority figures, thereby highlighting one category of people. Because the authorities were often harsh toward Christians, the believers may have been inclined to despise them and not pray for them. Perhaps the believers hoped that their persecutors would burn in hell forever. Paul, however, writes that God also wants prayers to be sent up for them. Why? Because God ". . . wants all men to be saved and to come to a knowledge of the truth." In other words, the gospel is also for those in positions of authority.

There is a beautiful thought pattern in this passage. Paul writes that there is one God (2:5), and we know from Scripture that this one God is the Maker of all people. Paul said to the Athenians that from one man God made every nation of men (Acts 17:26). God is the Maker of all people — of whatever race, colour, or social standing. And then Paul writes to Timothy that there is ". . . one Mediator between God and men, the man Christ Jesus, who gave himself as a ransom for all men" (2:5, 6). There is one God who made all men, and there is one Mediator between God and men. All men will only find salvation in this one Mediator! Notice that Paul identifies this one Mediator as "the *man* Christ Jesus." It does not matter whether we are of high or low standing in society, everyone belongs to mankind, and Christ Jesus came into this world as a man. The common denominator of all people is their humanity, and this is what the Son of God took upon Himself when He was born in Bethlehem! Paul even implies in 2:7 that this is why the gospel extended from the Jews to the Gentiles: all belong to the human race, and God wants all kinds of people to be saved.

Therefore, we confess in the Canons of Dort the following: "The promise of the gospel is that whoever believes in Christ crucified shall not perish but have eternal life. This promise ought to be announced and proclaimed universally and without discrimination to all peoples and to all men, to whom God in His good pleasure sends the gospel, together with the command to repent and believe" (ch. II art.5). The gospel must go to all kinds of people. Race, colour, cultural background, social standing, educational level, make no difference. And we must pray that God will bless this outreach! As far as the conversion of those in positions of government is concerned, this will have blessed consequences for the church because Paul speaks in passing about us living peaceful and quiet lives in all godliness and holiness (2:2).

Precisely because there is only eternal salvation through Jesus Christ, the gospel must be proclaimed universally. The gospel must be shared with politicians, yuppies, street people, Asians, Africans, Europeans, and everyone else. The Word tells us to pray that all kinds of people will embrace this gospel because there is one God, one Mediator, and one mankind!

Read: Hebrews 7:11-28

Jesus Lives to Intercede for Us

Therefore He is able to save completely those who come to God through Him, because He always lives to intercede for them.

Hebrews 7:25

Every year, the church commemorates the ascension of our Lord Jesus Christ into heaven. Ascension Day is not one of those cherished days on the Christian calendar such as Christmas, Good Friday, and Easter. We know that the birth of our Lord Jesus means that the Saviour came into the world, and we know that His death means that He took our sins upon Himself. We know that His resurrection means that He conquered sin and death. But what does the ascension of our Lord signify?

Concerning Christ's ascension into heaven, the Heidelberg Catechism identifies three benefits, of which the first is that ". . . He is our Advocate in heaven before His Father" (Lord's Day 18 Q&A 49). Indeed, the writer to the Hebrews says that we have a High Priest who is ". . . exalted above the heavens" (7:26) and who ". . . always lives to intercede for [us]" (7:25). Christ now applies the benefits of His death and resurrection to us by speaking on our behalf in the presence of His Father.

The Levitical priests were prevented by death from continuing in office, but Jesus has a permanent priesthood because He lives forever (7:23, 24). Notice that the writer uses the Name "Jesus" within this context (7:22), thereby pointing to the earthly ministry of our Saviour. This is the Name of which an angel said to Joseph in a dream, " . . . you are to give Him the Name Jesus, because He will save His people from their sins" (Mt 1:21). Because Jesus died but rose again, His priesthood is permanent and, as our ascended Saviour, He exercises His priesthood in the heavenly tabernacle. Jesus Christ sits at the

Father's right hand, where He intercedes for us. This is the flow of thought when the writer says, "*Therefore* He is able to save completely those who come to God through Him, *because* He always lives to intercede for them." Jesus Christ lives and therefore He acts as Saviour to this very day!

The Levitical priests appeared in the LORD's presence with the blood of goats and bulls, but Christ ". . . entered the Most Holy Place once for all by His own blood, having obtained eternal redemption" (Heb 9:12). On the basis of His own blood which He shed for us on the cross for the forgiveness of all our sins, the Lord Jesus Christ can intercede for us with the Father. When we come to God for the forgiveness of our sins in the Name of Jesus, the Saviour speaks on our behalf. When we pray to God in the Name of Jesus Christ, Christ intercedes for us. We can approach God and enter the heavenly throne room in prayer since we have a great High Priest in heaven (Heb 9:19-22).

This is a tremendous comfort for us when we approach God in true faith. Christ is able to save us completely because of His redeeming work on the cross, and He indeed intercedes for us with the Father to that effect. Sin was the great obstacle between us and God after the Fall, but Christ came to clear away the obstacle and reconcile us to the Father. We can again have fellowship with the Father.

There was a time when our accuser, the devil, spoke about us in the presence of the Father (cf. Job 1:6-11; 2:1-4). The devil entered the heavenly throne room to point out the weaknesses and sins of God's people, but after Christ's resurrection and ascension this is no longer possible (Rev 12:9, 10). There is no longer someone appearing before God to make a case *against* us, but there is Someone making a case *for* us! There is no longer an a*ccuser* in heaven, but an *Advocate*! As John writes, ". . . we have One who speaks to the Father in our defense — Jesus Christ, the Righteous One" (I Jn 2:1). The good news of Christ's ascension is that our High Priest intercedes for us as our Advocate in heaven. As such, the Lord Jesus Christ applies His redeeming work to us.

The wonderfully liberating message of the text is that salvation is guaranteed for us as believers because Jesus Christ lives to intercede for us. As Paul writes, ". . . there is now no condemnation for those who are in Christ Jesus . . ." (Rom 8:1). Complete and eternal salvation is guaranteed in Christ Jesus for believers!

Read: I John 1

God is Faithful and Just

If we confess our sins, He is faithful and just and will forgive us our sins and purify us from all unrighteousness.

I John 1:9

The Word of God teaches that we need self-knowledge — self-knowledge of the most important kind, namely, knowledge of our sin and misery. This does not mean that we attain this knowledge ourselves; in fact, only from the Word of God do we learn that we are sinners. Apart from God's revelation, we would not know our true natural *condition* (conceived and born in sin and inclined to all manner of evil), nor our true natural *status* (guilty and condemnable in the sight of God). Throughout our whole life we will have to deal with the reality of sin. Just before the text, John writes: "If we claim to be without sin, we deceive ourselves and the truth is not in us" (1:8).

Sometimes believers worry whether all their sins are really forgiven. Particularly a sin against which we must struggle time and again but do not seem to make much headway in overcoming, can make us wonder whether the Lord will really forgive us.

But then we may focus on the words of the text: "If we confess our sins, He is faithful and just and will forgive us our sins and purify us from all unrighteousness." John speaks about confessing our sins without going into details about what confession means, but you will understand that this is an honest confession made with integrity, which means that we have broken and contrite hearts and are heartily sorry for our sins and fight against them. God is not just interested in words, but in the attitude of the heart. John says that if we confess our sins, God is faithful and just and will forgive us our sins.

Notice carefully that John does not just say that if we confess our sins, God will forgive us our sins. John says: "If we confess our sins, *He is faithful and just* and will forgive us our sins and purify us from all unrighteousness." There is a *guarantee* for the forgiveness of our sins, and it lies in God's faithfulness and justice!

God is faithful — faithful to His promise of forgiveness! Scripture records in many places the promise of forgiveness; that promise even lies at the heart of the covenant. And we know from Scripture that God is faithful to His covenant promises. His words are spoken in truth, and stand forever! God faithfully keeps His promise of forgiveness because He is the faithful One!

God is also just — just in the sense that He does what is right and good. This is closely connected with God's faithfulness because if God says He will do something, it is a matter of His justice that He will then also do it. God sent His Son into this world to pay the price for our sins, and since the price has been paid, God, in His justice, will not exact the price from us. Christ bore the wrath of God against our sins so that we may be filled with God's blessing. Therefore, it is a matter of God's justice to grant us the blessing of forgiveness when we confess our sins.

Yes, in His faithfulness and justice, God will forgive us our sins and purify us from all unrighteousness. Therefore, the *guarantee* of our forgiveness lies in the very fact of who God is! He is the faithful and just One!

Forgiveness means that ". . . as far as the east is from the west, so far has He removed our transgressions from us" (Ps. 103:12). John uses a word for forgiveness which has as its root meaning the notion of "sending away." When we confess our sins, God removes our sins from His sight so that He does not focus on them; they have been paid for by the atoning sacrifice of Jesus Christ (cf. I Jn 2:2). God then applies to us the redeeming work of Christ. There is the reassuring aspect of finality in that word "forgiveness."

And God purifies us from all unrighteousness when we confess our sins. He washes us so that we are clean. When we are forgiven, our robes are white because they have been washed in the blood of the Lamb (Rev 7:14). We are then whiter than snow, not by nature but by virtue of Jesus Christ's work.

God looks at us as we are through faith in Jesus Christ. When we confess our sins, we are forgiven and purified people. That is a matter of God's covenant faithfulness and justice!

Read: Job 1

Praise the Lord in Adversity

At this, Job got up and tore his robe and shaved his head. Then he fell to the ground in worship and said: "Naked I came from my mother's womb, and naked I will depart. The Lord gave and the Lord has taken away; may the Name of the Lord be praised."

Job 1:20, 21

Often we take our health and prosperity for granted and expect the Lord to continue to give us many blessings. But sometimes the Lord withholds His blessings from us, with the result that we are plunged into adversity. How are we to react then? It is easy to praise the Lord when the Lord showers his blessings upon us, but what is our attitude toward the Lord in the face of adversity?

Job was a man who had everything. The Lord had blessed him with sons and daughters, as well as many animals. Job's wealth was so impressive that he is described as ". . . the greatest man among all the people of the East" (1:3). But then the Lord let Job be struck with disaster: in one day, Job lost all his animals and all his children. What a tragedy!

How did Job react? Job expressed his intense sorrow by tearing his robe and shaving his head, and then he fell to the ground in worship. Rather than curse God — as the devil thought Job would do (1:9-11) — Job continued to confess his faith in God. Job worshipped God!

Job confessed his own innate poverty with the moving words, "Naked I came from my mother's womb, and naked I will depart." Job knew that he had brought nothing into the world and that he would take nothing out of the world. This is a difficult confession for us to make because we are success-oriented and want to amass as many things as possible in this life. And yet, the reality of this confession puts many things in proper perspective.

Furthermore, Job also confessed God's sovereignty when he said, "The LORD gave and the LORD has taken away . . ." Job not only looked at himself, but he looked especially toward God in faith. We so easily question the fairness of a certain development and ask whether it was fair that Job had to suffer so much. We expect the LORD to give us good things and then complain when He takes them away from us. We so easily protest and rebel when God takes away a loved one or deprives us of possessions, and we try to fight against God. Perhaps we sometimes even come to the point of hating God and shaking our fist at heaven. The answer in such situations is that God is sovereign, and He has the right to do whatever pleases Him. We must learn to confess God's sovereignty in these matters: the LORD gives and the LORD takes away. Rather than fight the LORD, let us thank the LORD for the time that He did allow us to enjoy someone or something.

And then we will also be able to praise the Name of the LORD. Job said, ' . . . may the Name of the LORD be praised." Instead of protesting and rebelling against the LORD, Job praised the Name of the LORD in worship. Through his tears, Job praised the LORD! Job realized that there is more to life than the affliction that we may sometimes experience. Job knew the God of his life to be the God of grace. Although Job probably lived very early in the history of redemption, Job knew enough about the gospel of salvation to be comforted. Therefore, when Job himself was afflicted with a terrible sickness later, he exclaimed: "I know that my Redeemer lives, and that in the end He will stand upon the earth. And after my skin has been destroyed, yet in my flesh I will see God; I myself will see Him with my own eyes — I, and not another. How my heart yearns within me" (Job 19:25-27)! By the grace of God, Job had an eternal perspective on life and realized that the greatest treasure is the gospel of eternal salvation. There is much brokenness in this fallen world, but those who know the promise of the gospel have a perspective and hope which transcends this brokenness.

When disaster strikes us, there are only two possibilities: either we continue praising the LORD, or we curse the LORD. May God give us the grace to praise him even in adversity.

Read: Psalm 62

My Soul Finds Rest in God Alone

My soul finds rest in God alone; my salvation comes from Him. He alone is my rock and my salvation; He is my fortress, I will never be shaken.

Psalm 62:1, 2

Have you ever felt like a tottering fence? Sometimes we face hardships in life which weigh so heavily upon us that we feel like we are going to fall over. This is how David felt when he wrote this Psalm.

As with many of the Psalms, we do not know the specific circumstances under which this Psalm was written. Maybe David was already king, given that verse 4 says, "They fully intend to topple him from his lofty place . . ." Maybe David was not yet king but already anointed to be king, which was a lofty position in itself. Regardless of the specific circumstances, David was under intense pressure and he felt as if he was going to collapse, like a fence totters after years of wear and eventually collapses.

But David begins this Psalm with the wonderful confession that his soul finds rest in God alone because God is his rock and fortress. Because David knows who God is for him, David is at rest. He does not have to be agitated and anxious, because God is with him even in the midst of upsetting circumstances which press down upon him.

Why could David be at rest? David answers this when he says, ". . . my salvation comes from Him," and David elaborates on this when he says, "He alone is my rock and my salvation; He is my fortress, I will never be shaken." The LORD would deliver David. How could David be so sure of this? The LORD had promised David at the time of his anointing that he would be king over Israel, and the LORD is faithful to His word. God had a purpose for David among His people as God worked out

His plan of redemption, and David could be assured that no matter what hardships he had to endure he would not be toppled. This became even more clear later when the LORD told David that his house and his kingdom would endure forever and that his throne would be established forever (II Sam 7:16). Ultimately this promise would be fulfilled in Jesus Christ, the Saviour King who came from the line of David and was born in the city of David. As the angel Gabriel said to Mary about the Child to whom she would give birth, "The Lord God will give Him the throne of His father David, and He will reign over the house of Jacob forever; His kingdom will never end" (Lk 1:32, 33). Therefore, we know, even more clearly than David may have known, why God would not let him be shaken. Any attack on David was essentially an attack on God's work of salvation, and therefore it could but only fail.

And why can we be at rest? We too can find rest in the LORD's work of salvation because God unfailingly works out His plan of salvation in our lives. God's ultimate purpose for our lives is that we are saved from sin and misery and will dwell with Him forever in blessed fellowship. Whatever may totter and collapse in the lives of believers, this reality will always remain standing. Apart from this knowledge, there is no rest during times of turmoil. We find rest in the Apostle Paul's formulation of what David is essentially saying: "And we know that in all things God works for the good of those who love Him, who have been called according to His purpose" (Rom 8:28). And Paul concludes by saying: "For I am convinced that neither death nor life, neither angels nor demons, neither the present nor the future, nor any powers, neither height nor depth, nor anything else in all creation, will be able to separate us from the love of God that is in Christ Jesus our Lord" (Rom 8:38, 39).

Indeed, as we face various hardships of life, we find rest in the reality of our salvation. David even uses a word for "salvation" which is closely related to our Saviour's Name. It is a word similar to the Hebrew name "Joshua," which means "the

LORD saves," from which the Name "Jesus" is derived. My soul finds rest in God alone because He is my Saviour!

Therefore we may boldly confess that God is our rock and fortress. We sometimes say that someone is our "Rock of Gibraltar," meaning that we have a rock-solid and immovable person on whom we can lean in times of trouble. God is our "Rock of Gibraltar." Moreover, as a fortress offers safety and security because it is a place of refuge, so we find refuge in God. God is our fortress. Life's storms and tempests may cause upheaval in our lives, but God our Saviour is our rock and fortress. Today we may find rest in God, knowing that we are headed toward the eternal rest where we will never feel as if we are tottering.

Read: Psalm 135

The LORD is Great!

I know that the LORD is great, that our Lord is greater than all gods. The LORD does whatever pleases Him, in the heavens and on the earth, in the seas and all their depths.

Psalm 135:5, 6

The Psalmist makes a very personal confession of faith when he says, "*I* know that the LORD is great, that our Lord is greater than all gods." We do not know who the author of this Psalm is, nor do we know when he lived, but we do know his personal conviction. As a member of God's covenant people, he composed this Psalm and draws God's people into his own personal confession when he says, "I know . . . that *our* Lord is greater than all gods." God is not just his personal Lord but Israel's Lord. By writing this Psalm, the author put his own confession on the lips of all God's people. We too can say, "The LORD is great!"

We are God's people and may confess great things about Him because He has revealed Himself to us as the great God. The Psalmist says, "The LORD does whatever pleases Him, in the heavens and on the earth, in the seas and all their depths." The greatness of our God is that He does whatever pleases Him. And God does this everywhere, because the Psalmist mentions the heavens, the earth, the sea, and the depths of the sea. God does whatever pleases Him in the entire universe!

Essentially the Psalmist is confessing God's greatness in light of His providence over all things. The Heidelberg Catechism, Lord's Day 10, captures well what this means: "God's providence is His almighty and ever present power, whereby, as with His hand, He still upholds heaven and earth and all creatures, and so governs them that leaf and blade, rain and drought, fruitful and barren years, food and drink, health and sickness, riches and poverty, indeed, all things, come to us not by chance but by His fatherly hand" (Q&A 27).

To show this, the Psalmist refers first to the world of creation, when he says that the LORD ". . . makes clouds rise from the ends of the earth; He sends lightning with the rain and brings out the wind from His storehouses" (135:7). Perhaps we do not often think about the LORD when considering the so-called natural phenomena, but they do not come *naturally*! Everything comes from God's hand.

Also the events happening on the earth come from the LORD's hand because the Psalmist says that "The LORD does whatever pleases Him . . . *on the earth.*" Evidence of the LORD's greatness is that through world events the LORD is working out His plan of salvation. The Psalmist points out major events in the history of redemption by stating, "He struck down the firstborn of Egypt, the firstborn of men and animals. He sent his signs and wonders into your midst, O Egypt, against Pharaoh and all his servants. He struck down many nations and killed mighty kings — Sihon king of the Amorites, Og king of Bashan and all the kings of Canaan — and He gave their land as an inheritance, an inheritance to His people Israel" (135:8-12). In these few short verses, the Psalmist highlights the major events of Israel's early history, namely, the exodus, the wilderness wanderings, and the conquest of Canaan. By all these events in the history of redemption, the LORD shows that He is great!

Also today, the LORD continues to work out the same plan of redemption because ". . . the LORD will vindicate His people and have compassion on His servants" (135:14). We may be assured that the history of redemption continues until the LORD has reached the culmination of His saving purpose through the redeeming work of Jesus Christ. Christ will return to inaugurate the new earth where God will dwell with His people forever. Wars, political upheaval, diplomatic developments, economic situations, and personal well-being are all in God's hand and have a place in His plan of redemption. Therefore, as the

Heidelberg Catechism states in Lord's Day 10, ". . . with a view to the future we can have firm confidence in our faithful God and Father that no creature shall separate us from His love; for all creatures are so completely in His hand that without His will they cannot so much as move" (Q&A 28).

This Psalm shows the LORD's greatness by pointing to the world of creation and the work of redemption. The God who provides us with our food and drink is the God who also makes provision for our eternal salvation. If we see this clearly, we will also confess that God makes all things work together for the good of those who love Him, that is, for the good of their eternal salvation (Heidelberg Catechism, Lord's Day 1 Q&A 1). Rain and drought, health and sickness, riches and poverty, peace and war — all have a place in God's eternal plan for the salvation of His people.

The Psalmist says that the LORD is ". . . greater than all gods," and he shows the uselessness of the idols by describing them as mere images made by the hands of men (135:16, 17). Today the western world does not have such idols, but the western world does have other idols which are just as much fashioned by man: technology, money, celebrities, and sports icons. Let us not put our trust in the idols of man because the gods of the nations are no gods, and the LORD can throw a wrench into all human efforts.

The LORD is great! Therefore, the Psalm begins and ends by saying, "Praise the LORD!"

Read: Psalm 146

Blessed is He whose Help
is the God of Jacob

Blessed is he whose help is the God of Jacob, whose hope is in the LORD his God, the Maker of heaven and earth, the sea, and everything in them — the LORD, who remains faithful forever.

Psalm 146:5, 6

We often put our trust in powerful people, but this Psalm teaches us that they are but "mortal men" (146:3). The movers and shakers of this world can make many plans, but all it takes is for them to stop breathing and their plans come to nothing. The capabilities of people are limited because people are not divine. Every living person — no matter how powerful — is only a breath away from death! Therefore, we are told, "Do not put your trust in princes, in mortal men, who cannot save" (146:3).

Instead, we are truly blessed when our help is the God of Jacob, the Maker of heaven and earth. Over against the bleak description of man is the description of God in all His divine power because the Psalmist refers to God as ". . . the Maker of heaven and earth, the sea, and everything in them . . ." God's power is nowhere so evident as in the creation of this world. The Apostle Paul writes that ". . . since the creation of the world God's invisible qualities — His eternal power and divine nature — have been clearly seen, being understood from what has been made . . ." (Rom 1:20). We also confess in the first article of the Apostles' Creed, "I believe in God the Father *almighty*, Creator of heaven and earth." The LORD has the power to help in time of need! Whether we are faced with sickness, financial worries, oppression, or other adversities, the LORD has the power to help. As almighty God, the LORD is able to provide us with all the things we need for body and soul and to turn to our good whatever adversity He sends us (Heidelberg Catechism, Lord's Day 9 Q&A 26).

Not only does the Psalmist speak about God's power, but he also points to God's faithfulness. This powerful God is the God of the covenant and, therefore, He is faithful to His people. The One who made heaven and earth is ". . . the LORD, who remains faithful forever." Notice that the Psalmist speaks about *the LORD* — thereby using God's covenant Name — and he does so no less than twelve times in this short Psalm. This is the Name which in Hebrew ("Yahweh") literally means "I am who I am" and indicates that God is faithful to His covenant promises and will be there for His people. The LORD is who He says He is and does what He says He will do. In the history of Israel, the Name "Yahweh" was always associated with the LORD's faithfulness to His covenant promises. Contrast that with people. How many times has someone we know not promised to do something and then not done it? Or how often have we not been disappointed by people who we thought would certainly come through and help us? But thankfully the Bible teaches us that this is not the case with our LORD.

For this reason, the Psalmist says, "Blessed is he whose help is the God of Jacob, whose hope is in the LORD his God . . ." It is a tremendous blessing that God has incorporated us into His covenant of grace and promises to be as a Father to us. Rather than set our hearts on mortal men, we may set our hearts on the LORD God.

The LORD's activity on behalf of His people is a continuous activity. In the verses which give evidence of the LORD's power and faithfulness in the lives of His people (146:7-9), the Psalmist repeatedly uses a form of the verb which points to ongoing action. The LORD is continuously busy upholding the cause of the oppressed, giving food to the hungry, lifting up those bowed down, and sustaining the fatherless and the widow.

But does the LORD really always do those things? Sometimes God's children go hungry, suffer from serious illnesses, or are bowed down with various worries. Who has not seen the vivid and disturbing photos on the news of malnourished children, or read about Christians persecuted for their faith? This leads some of God's people to ask in despair, "What help?"

We should realize that the Psalmist does not say that God *always* grants relief *in this life*. We may not take this Psalm in isolation from the rest of Scripture which clearly teaches that sometimes the LORD sends adversity. However, we may cling to the fact that ". . . God is *faithful*; He will not let you be tempted beyond what you can bear. But when you are tempted, He will also provide a way out so that you can stand up under it" (I Cor 10:13). Also in this way, God helps His people. That has been a tremendous comfort for many of God's children, and they have experienced the reality of those words. Furthermore, we may know that when God does send adversity, He does so for the good of our eternal salvation because He is preparing us for the new earth (Rom 8:28). Let us not focus on short-term temporal help, as important as that is in our life here on earth, but focus instead on the eternal blessedness that God is preparing. The miracles which our Lord Jesus Christ performed — the blind receiving sight, the lame walking, the lepers being cured, and the deaf hearing (Mt 11:5) — foreshadowed the blessedness of the new earth where God's children may enjoy the benefits of the covenant in full measure.

"Blessed is he whose help is the God of Jacob . . . the LORD, who remains faithful forever."

Read: Proverbs 3:1-8

Trust in the LORD *Always*

Trust in the LORD *with all your heart and lean not on your own understanding; in all your ways acknowledge Him, and He will make your paths straight.*

Proverbs 3:5, 6

By nature we are inclined to trust in ourselves and to lean on our own understanding. We want to be the master of our own lives, without regard for God. That was precisely the sin of Adam and Eve, our first parents in paradise, who were led to believe by the devil that they could rely on their own understanding and live independently of God. Ever since that time, the call has gone out to trust in the LORD and acknowledge Him in everything that we do.

Of course, the text does not mean that we may not use our understanding, since God gives us the gift of understanding for use in His service. The book of Proverbs shows clearly that man should use his understanding to develop skills and get ahead in life. The text says that we may not *lean on* our own understanding and *rely on* it as if we ourselves can chart the course of our lives. Someone who leans on a cane to get around depends on that cane; it is his support. The LORD, however, does not want us to depend on our own insight, but instead He wants us to depend on Him.

Notice that the text speaks about trusting in *the LORD*, thereby using God's covenant Name. We are told to trust in Him who has made an eternal covenant of grace with us and has promised to provide us with all good and avert all evil or turn it to our benefit. Throughout the history of redemption, the LORD has been faithful to His covenant promises. At the fullness of time, the Father sent the promised Saviour and thus the foundation was laid for covenant fellowship. Christ is our wisdom from God, that is, our righteousness, holiness, and redemption (I Cor 1:30). The wisdom of God pertains to that which no human mind could conceive, namely, salvation through Jesus Christ! Therefore, in every other aspect of life too, we should not rely on our own understanding.

Our faithful covenant God asks for the response of faith from us! This involves a radical demand: "Trust in the LORD with *all* your heart . . . ; in *all* your ways acknowledge Him . . ." The LORD is telling us that He wants our undivided hearts. Yet, it is a daily struggle for us to place all our trust in God because we so easily fall into the trap of relying first on ourselves and on God for only a few areas of our lives. Sometimes we think and act as if God is for the soul and the rest is our business. This is far from the truth! Rather than being removed from daily affairs, God is so involved that He even knows the number of the hairs on our head (Mt 10:30). God wants us to recognize that He has an absolute claim on our lives and that He must be acknowledged in everything that we undertake. Just as it is insulting to someone when we ignore that person and do not acknowledge his presence, so it is insulting to God when we ignore Him and do not acknowledge His presence in our lives. The LORD wants us to ask what is right and pleasing according to Him, thereby acknowledging that we are dependent on His help in everything that we do.

Sometimes we look at people who live without God, and we think that they are managing just fine. Perhaps it even looks attractive to live like they do, without regard for God and without any apparent limitations. But the book of Proverbs points out that living without God is self-destructive ultimately since "The LORD's curse is on the house of the wicked, but He blesses the home of the righteous" (Prov 3:33).

When we trust in the LORD and acknowledge Him in all our ways, we will be rewarded because the LORD will make our paths straight. This does not mean that life will be free of problems. In fact, sometimes life seems as if it is full of zigzags and detours brought about by various adversities. Yet, through it all, the LORD is working out His plan of salvation for our lives. As the Apostle Paul says, ". . . in all things God works for the good of those who love Him, who have been called according to His purpose" (Rom 8:28; cf. Heidelberg Catechism, Lord's Day 1 Q&A 1). We will arrive at the goal for our lives: blessed fellowship with God in glory!

Read: Proverbs 16:1-9

We Plan but the LORD Determines our Steps

In his heart a man plans his course, but the LORD determines his steps.

Proverbs 16:9

We like to plan our lives by thinking things through and taking initiatives. And that is a good thing. If we did not plan, we would not accomplish much and would not function well in our God-given position of stewards over His gifts. The book of Proverbs has much good to say about making plans.

But this text keeps us humble because it contains a contrast: "In his heart a man plans his course, but the LORD determines his steps." There is a difference between planning and planning. Our planning must always be within the framework of dependence upon the LORD. This is difficult for us to accept because by nature we can all be classified as "control freaks" — people who want to be in control. By nature, we want to chart the course of our own lives. Was this not the very sin of Adam and Eve, our first parents in paradise? They fell for the temptation of the devil that they did not have to be dependent upon God and could chart the direction of their own lives.

The text teaches that we are dependent upon the LORD and must therefore be humble before the LORD. We must always remember what we confess in Lord's Day 10 of the Heidelberg Catechism: ". . . all creatures are so completely in [God's] hand that without His will they cannot so much as move" (Q&A 28). James writes, "Now listen, you who say, 'Today or tomorrow we will go to this or that city, spend a year there, carry on business and make money.' . . . Instead, you ought to say, 'If it is the Lord's will, we will live and do this or that' " (Jms 4:13, 15).

And Proverbs also says, "Do not boast about tomorrow, for you do not know what a day may bring forth" (Prov 27:1). The doctrine of God's providence is that the LORD determines man's steps.

Is this frustrating? For unbelievers, yes, such a doctrine is frustrating. As believers, we too can easily be frustrated when things do not happen the way we planned, because by nature we want to be in control. Nevertheless, we may derive great comfort from the fact that God determines our steps. In article 13 of the Belgic Confession, we confess about the doctrine of God's providence: "This doctrine gives us unspeakable consolation, for we learn thereby that nothing can happen to us by chance, but only by the direction of our gracious heavenly Father." God's involvement in our daily lives is so great that He even knows the number of the hairs on our head (Mt 10:30). Therefore, with respect to the doctrine that God upholds all things by His providence, the Heidelberg Catechism says that ". . . with a view to the future we can have a firm confidence in our faithful God and Father that no creature shall separate us from His love" (Lord's Day 10 Q&A 28). We do not know what the future will bring, but we do know that the LORD directs the steps of His children and that He does so with their eternal salvation in mind.

Notice carefully that the text speaks about *the LORD* directing man's steps. The author uses God's covenant Name — "Yahweh" — which means "I am who I am." It is the Name which points to God's covenant faithfulness: He is who He says He is, and He fulfils His covenant promises. For believers, this is tremendously comforting because the LORD determines our steps in faithfulness to His covenant promises!

And what is God's promise for His faithful children? Eternal salvation! In Lord's Day 1 of the Heidelberg Catechism, we confess that ". . . without the will of my heavenly Father not a hair can fall from my head; indeed, all things must work together *for my salvation*" (Q&A 1). God's covenant promises all centre around Jesus Christ, whom God the Father sent into the world to deliver people from the dominion of sin and death.

This is what we must remember when our plans do not always materialize as we would like. Man plans, but the LORD determines and directs. What a blessing, however, that God determines our steps! What we think is good for us is perhaps not good for us at all. God sees the whole picture and knows what is best for us, keeping in mind that the great goal for our lives is eternal salvation. God is preparing us for entrance into his glorious presence, and He puts our feet on the path of salvation.

Knowing this framework wards off frustration. Things may not go as we would like, but things are in God's hands. He knows best. Our plans may not materialize, in fact our lives may seem to be disintegrating, but what counts is that God's plan of salvation materializes. At the same time, knowing this framework teaches us to trust in the LORD and to walk with Him in humble submission.

Read: Isaiah 46

The Lord Carries His People

*Listen to Me, O house of Jacob, all you who remain of
the house of Israel, you whom I have upheld since you
were conceived, and have carried since your birth.
Even to your old age and gray hairs I am He, I am He
who will sustain you. I have made you and I will carry
you; I will sustain you and I will rescue you.*

Isaiah 46:3, 4

The Lord sent Isaiah to Judah with the message that Judah
was going to go into captivity because of its unfaithfulness to
the Lord. However, the Lord not only sent Isaiah with a message
of doom but also with a message of hope. The Lord would not
totally abandon His people; a remnant would return from exile.
The Lord would be faithful to His covenant promises made to
their forefather Abraham.

The second half of the book of Isaiah is sometimes called
the book of comfort, beginning with the Lord's well-known and
beloved words to Isaiah, "Comfort, comfort my people, says
your God" (Is 40:1). The Lord commissioned Isaiah to tell Judah
what would happen to the Babylonians after they had taken Judah
into exile. The Babylonians themselves would be conquered by
a stronger superpower; the Lord would cause the Persian ruler
Cyrus to strike a devastating blow against the Babylonians (Is
45:1-6). And Cyrus would allow a remnant to return to Jerusalem.
In this way, the Lord provided comfort and hope for His people.

As the Babylonians faced this impending crisis, their gods
would be of no help to them. Bel and Nebo — the main
Babylonian gods — would not be able to protect the Babylonians.
In the mad flight away from the Persians, the images of these
gods would be loaded on oxen and mules and hauled away. The
images would stoop and bow as the animals stooped and bowed

along the way, and the gods represented by the images would not even be able to rescue the burden. Because they are no gods, the Babylonian gods would be powerless.

The LORD contrasts these false gods with Himself. This contrast would be Judah's comfort. The Babylonians would have to carry their own gods, but the LORD carries His people! The LORD says that He has upheld His people since they were conceived and that He has carried them since their birth. And the LORD would continue to do so. "Even to your old age and gray hairs I am He, I am He who will sustain you."

What a comforting reality for God's people of all times and places! God carries us from conception to death — and beyond! Yes, also beyond death because the LORD says, "I will sustain you and I will rescue you." For Judah, this meant that there would be deliverance from exile, but this deliverance from exile foreshadowed the redeeming work of Jesus Christ. In Jesus Christ, the LORD has made provision for the ultimate deliverance and salvation of His people. The LORD carries His people into eternity!

The LORD uses beautiful imagery which underscores the great privilege of belonging to Him: the LORD carries His people as a father carries his child. The comparison which the LORD makes with the false gods also contains the implicit warning that those who do not serve the LORD do not have this comfort. If we create our own gods, we will have to carry those gods ourselves; gods of our own making will not be able to carry us. If we make an idol of work, money, drugs and alcohol, or sex, we will have to carry those things on our own shoulders as a heavy burden. Although those things may give us some temporary pleasure, they will not be able to carry us through life. We will eventually stagger under their weight — certainly as we approach death's door. God wants us to understand this clearly, and He wants us to build our lives on the comfort of His covenant promises. That is why the LORD says, "Listen to Me, O house of Jacob . . ."

The L ord's words spoken through Isaiah remind us of what David says: "Yet You brought me out of the womb; You made me trust in You even at my mother's breast. From birth I was cast upon You; from my mother's womb You have been my God" (Ps. 22:9, 10). And it reminds us of these words of David: "The L ord will fulfil His purpose for me; Your love, O L ord, endures forever . . ." (Ps. 138:8). As believers, we may confess that God is carrying us in such a way that He makes all things work for the good of our salvation (Heidelberg Catechism, Lord's Day 1 Q&A 1).

Read: Acts 7:54 - 8:8

Christ is in Control

On that day a great persecution broke out against the church at Jerusalem, and all except the apostles were scattered throughout Judea and Samaria . . . Those who had been scattered preached the Word wherever they went.

Acts 8:1b, 4

Sometimes we wonder about the purpose of things happening in our personal lives or in the world at large. Sickness, financial hardship, terrorist attacks, wars and natural disasters can make us wonder whether there is any direction to events. The Word of God teaches that Christ is in control and that He is guiding all things for the completion of the plan of redemption (Eph 1:20-22). But what do we see of it?

Luke begins the Book of Acts by indicating that he is going to write about the things that Jesus Christ did after His ascension into heaven (cf. Acts 1:1, 2) in order to show that Christ uses His power from heaven for the benefit of the gospel's spread throughout the world. As such, the Book of Acts is not so much about the acts of the apostles as about the acts of the ascended Christ!

We see something of Christ's control in the events soon after Pentecost, as revealed in the text. Before His ascension into heaven, Christ had told His apostles that they should wait in Jerusalem for the outpouring of the Holy Spirit (Acts 1:4). Christ told them that they would receive power when the Holy Spirit had come upon them, and they would be His witnesses ". . . in Jerusalem, and in all Judea and Samaria, and to the ends of the earth" (Acts 1:8). Thus Christ outlined the program for the spread of the gospel after Pentecost: first Jerusalem, then Judea and Samaria, and then the ends of the earth. Acts 8:1b and 4 show us how Christ *implemented* part of this program for the spread of the gospel: believers from Jerusalem were scattered throughout the region of Judea and Samaria as a result of a persecution, and those who were scattered preached the Word wherever they went. Note well that Christ used a persecution to move from the first phase to the second phase of the spread of the gospel. The gospel's rejection by Jerusalem had been sealed with the martyrdom of Stephen, who was stoned to death (7:59, 60). Now it was time for the gospel to go to Judea and Samaria, and Christ used for His own purpose the subsequent persecution which broke out "on that day."

The gospel of the risen and exalted Christ came to Judea and Samaria in the time after Pentecost because those who were scattered from Jerusalem preached the Word wherever they went. One could also translate that they *evangelized*. When people asked them why they were fleeing, they had an opportunity to testify about Christ. While it may have looked like the cause of the gospel was being shattered in Jerusalem by the persecution, the persecution actually served to spread the gospel! In this way, Christ was preparing the ground for His apostles to move beyond Jerusalem in their task of proclaiming the gospel. For notice also that the apostles were not scattered, a detail which is evidence of Christ's complete control in these events.

Christ works in unexpected ways. Even when we are not able to discern a guiding hand in events, Christ is working out the plan of redemption. The believers in Jerusalem who had to endure persecution probably had many questions because they did not see the overall picture, but this did not mean that there was no overall picture. This snapshot in the history of the church has been revealed to us to make clear that Christ is in control, even though this may not be readily evident to our eyes. This should give us tremendous comfort. Personal hardship, wars, and natural disasters serve a purpose in the coming of God's kingdom. God can draw us closer to the Word by means of difficulties in our personal lives, and terrible events on a world-scale can provide openings for the spread of the gospel. May the words of this text comfort us as we live in a dark world, or if we have to face difficult circumstances in our own lives. Christ rules on high and is directing all things for the completion of the plan of redemption!

Read: Ecclesiastes 1:1-11

Your Labour in the Lord is Not in Vain

Therefore, my dear brothers, stand firm. Let nothing move you. Always give yourselves fully to the work of the Lord, because you know that your labor in the Lord is not in vain.

I Corinthians 15:58

In North America, we are familiar with Labour Day, the first Monday in September which is set aside for celebrating the achievements of the labour movement for the benefit of working men and women. Its focus is very man-centered and materialistic. As Christians, do we ever reflect on the value of all our work? The Apostle Paul writes that our labour in the Lord is not in vain. This statement is truly gospel — good news in a fallen world — because apart from this reality our labour has no value.

The book of Ecclesiastes offers a glimpse into the state of things apart from the gospel. It teaches that apart from Jesus Christ's redeeming work there is no sense of meaningful purpose and direction in all our labour. The author, who was a teacher in Israel, states his conclusion up front: " 'Meaningless! Meaningless!' says the Teacher. 'Utterly meaningless! Everything is meaningless' " (1:2). Man works hard, but "What does man gain from all his labor at which he toils under the sun" (1:3)? "All of it is meaningless, a chasing after the wind" (Eccl 2:17). And after someone has come to the end of his life, he must leave the fruit of his labour to another person (Eccl 2:18-20). As this teacher says, generations come and go with the rhythm of the rising and setting sun, the wind blowing back and forth, and the streams flowing in circles (1:4-7). Morever, who will remember the achievements of past generations (1:9-11)? Therefore, secular man questions the gain of endless toil. And who hasn't thought these very thoughts at the end of a tedious day or as that mountain of unfinished work looms day after day?

This description of labour in Ecclesiastes echoes what the LORD said in Genesis 3 about toiling in the sweat of one's brow among thorns and thistles after the Fall into sin. But this man is a teacher in Israel and he knows the promise of the gospel: a Saviour would come to bring salvation from sin and all the burdens of life in a fallen world! Therefore, by offering a glimpse of life apart from the gospel, the book of Ecclesiastes actually calls out for the coming Saviour!

The cry " 'Everything is meaningless'" (1:2) finds an answer in I Corinthians 15:58 because Paul says that ". . . your labor in the Lord is not in vain." Paul uses a word for *labour* which indicates its toilsome character. Our sweat and tears are not in vain because the Lord Jesus Christ arose from the dead, thereby opening up access to a new world. Christ died for our sins but arose from the grave, and now sin and death no longer have us in their grip (I Cor 15:3, 17). If Christ had not been raised from the dead, we would still be in our sins and we would face the fearful prospect of eternal condemnation. Then all our labour would be in vain and Ecclesiastes' cry about meaninglessness would ring true for all of us. But, as it is, our labour in the Lord is not in vain! Its value will endure because it will redound to God's glory into eternity. We may believe that there is an inheritance for those who receive the gospel of Jesus Christ in true faith. Christ's physical resurrection from the dead is central to our eternal hope and we must cling to this fact, especially at a time when so many reject this doctrine.

Furthermore, because we know that our labour in the Lord is not in vain, Paul says, "Always give yourselves fully to the work of the Lord . . ." What work does Paul mean? Work in the church? That is certainly included. We must be dedicated in spreading the gospel to outsiders, instructing the youth of the church in the doctrine of God's Word, comforting and admonishing the members of the congregation, and all the other work that occurs in the church. But Paul is referring to something broader than that because all our work is *labour in the Lord.* Elsewhere Paul writes, "*Whatever you do,* work at it with all your heart, as working for the Lord, not for men, since you know that you will receive an inheritance from the Lord as a reward. It is the Lord Christ you are serving" (Col 3:23, 24). The LORD mandated us at the very beginning of this world to subdue the earth, that is, to develop it to His glory (Gen 1:28). Through the redeeming work of Jesus Christ, we can begin to carry out this mandate, although it will be tough because of the effects of the Fall into sin. There may be much drudgery in our work, but we must maintain the perspective that it is ultimately for the Lord.

The Spirit as Deposit

Now it is God who has made us for this very purpose and has given us the Spirit as a deposit, guaranteeing what is to come.

II Corinthians 5:5

Believers look forward to the day of full salvation when Jesus Christ will return on the clouds of heaven and all things will be made new. Then we will receive glorified bodies, free from the effects of the Fall into sin. But what comfort do we have in the meantime? What guarantee do we have that all this will happen? The Apostle Paul writes that God has given us the Spirit as a deposit, guaranteeing what is to come.

The Lord Jesus Christ came into this world to lay the foundation for a glorious new life for us by His death and resurrection. After conquering sin and death, our Saviour ascended into heaven where He took His place at the Father's right hand. Christ's first major act after His ascension was that He poured out the Holy Spirit upon the church to dwell in the hearts of God's children. When we think about the outpouring of the Holy Spirit on the day of Pentecost, we should not only think about the fact that the Spirit dwells in our hearts to transform our lives but also that the Spirit dwells in us as a guarantee of what is to come. God promises us a glorious future, and Paul literally writes in verse 5, "Now it is God who has *prepared* us for this very purpose, *having given us the Spirit as a deposit*." Paul uses the language of business. Just like someone makes a downpayment on a purchase, thereby guaranteeing that the rest of the money will be paid, so God has given us the Spirit as a downpayment of what is to come. We have Someone from heaven dwelling in us as a guarantee of what is still to come from heaven.

This is meant to be of great comfort to us as we live in a fallen and broken world. In chapter 4, Paul writes about the hardships which he experienced as a servant of the gospel, even being in danger of death (II Cor 4:8-11). But Paul writes about an eternal glory that far outweighs all those hardships (II Cor 4:16-18). Although our circumstances are different because we do not presently face the possibility of death due to persecution, we are faced with the brokenness of life in other ways. We do face the possibility of death due to sickness and accidents. Some of us even live with very debilitating illnesses for years before our death. In such circumstances, we have the comfort of knowing that there is a glorious future for God's children, a future guaranteed by the indwelling of the Holy Spirit.

Paul writes, "Now we know that if the earthly tent we live in is destroyed, we have a building from God, an eternal house in heaven, not built by human hands" (5:1). Paul contrasts the *earthly tent* and the *building from God.* Since the former refers to the earthly body (cf. II Pt 1:13, 14), the latter refers to the glorified body prepared for us in Christ Jesus. Our earthly body is a temporary abode just like a tent is something we do not live in permanently, but the glorified body is a permanent abode just like a building and a house are permanent structures. The new body is a gift from God and will come down from heaven when Christ returns. This is our comfort when the earthly tent is destroyed by death, and God has even prepared us for this by giving us the Spirit as a deposit.

But since the time has not yet come, Paul speaks about longing for the glorified body while still in this fallen and broken world (5:2-4). Paul writes literally, "Meanwhile we groan, longing to be *clothed over* with our heavenly dwelling . . ." (5:2). Rather than experience death and decay, believers prefer to be *clothed over* with the glorified body. We want Christ to return during our lifetime so that we can be changed in the twinkling of an eye (cf. I Cor 15:51, 52). We do not want to be found unclothed and naked but still clothed, that is, still in the earthly tent (5:3, 4). Then the new body can simply be put over the old body like an overcoat is put over a suit jacket. That is the longing of Christians groaning in a broken world.

Paul goes on to write that, as much as we may desire to be alive at Christ's return, we also know that as long as we are at home in the body we are away from the Lord (5:6-8). Being away from the body, or being out of the earthly tent, means being at home with the Lord. Although death is an unpleasant reality, it is the entrance into Christ's presence (cf. Heidelberg Catechism, Lord's Day 16 Q&A 42). Thus we are comforted concerning death. And the indwelling of the Spirit comforts believers in the face of death because God has given us a deposit guaranteeing what is to come. Although we must go through death, our soul will be re-united with our body when Christ returns.

Whether we are alive when Christ returns or have already died and are no longer in the earthly tent, we have the comfort that we will receive a glorified body, an eternal house built by God. We may be confident because God has given us the Spirit as a deposit, guaranteeing what is to come!

Think and Act as Christians

Finally, brothers, whatever is true, whatever is noble, whatever is right, whatever is pure, whatever is lovely, whatever is admirable — if anything is excellent or praiseworthy — think about such things. Whatever you have learned or received or heard from me, or seen in me — put it into practice. And the God of peace will be with you.

Philippians 4:8, 9

Taken out of context, these qualities could be viewed as a list of humanistic principles prevalent in the Greek society of which Philippi was a part. The Greek society valued what is true, noble, right, pure, lovely, and admirable — as does our present humanistic Western world. But Paul is referring to something much deeper because he is writing within the context of the gospel. He writes these words to the Philippians because of their ". . . partnership in the gospel . . ." (Php 1:5).

Knowing the gospel of Jesus Christ crucified and risen gives an entirely new focus to our lives. As Paul writes in II Corinthians 5:17, ". . . if anyone is in Christ, he is a new creation . . ." Paul reminds his readers of this fact. He says: "Whatever happens, conduct yourselves in a manner worthy of the gospel of Christ" (Php 1:27). We are to live as Christians. After mentioning the Christian qualities of love and humility, Paul says, "Your attitude should be the same as that of Christ Jesus . . ." (Php 2:5). Within this context of the gospel, Paul tells us to focus on whatever is excellent or praiseworthy.

Having come to the end of his letter, Paul gives as broad and comprehensive an instruction as he can in these verses. We are to think about ". . . *whatever* is true, *whatever* is noble, *whatever* is right, *whatever* is pure, *whatever* is lovely, *whatever* is admirable . . ." Above all, this means that we are to reflect on the redeeming work of our Lord and Saviour Jesus Christ because this is the basis for everything that Paul writes in his letter. The gospel of salvation by grace through faith gives us the reason for focussing on what is pure and lovely. We must live in thankfulness for Christ's redeeming work and therefore focus on what is pleasing to God. Whatever we think, say, and do should be done out of true faith, in accordance with God's law, and to God's glory (Heidelberg Catechism, Lord's Day 33 Q&A 91).

Our whole life must bear the stamp of the gospel, and this means that all our thoughts must be in harmony with the gospel. There ought not to be any discrepancy between the Christian faith which we profess and how and what we think. This is why Paul also writes, "And this is my prayer: that your love may abound more and more in knowledge and depth of insight, so that you may be able to discern what is best and may be pure and blameless until the day of Christ . . ." (Php 1:9, 10).

This means that the standard for our lives as Christians is God's holy and perfect law. God himself has revealed to us what is true, noble, right, pure, lovely, and admirable. The Lord Jesus Christ, our chief Prophet and Teacher, has revealed to us the depth of God's law throughout His entire ministry on this earth. Recall the well-known Sermon on the Mount, in which Christ analyzed the depth of God's law by penetrating to the thoughts of man's heart. It should become second nature for us to always ask what is right and pleasing in the eyes of the Lord.

This was what the Philippians had learned from Paul, and this was what they had seen in Paul's own life. Paul now commands them — and us — to put it into practice. Paul tells us to make whatever is pleasing to the Lord the focus of our thoughts. Furthermore, not only must we engage in such thinking, we must also act according to it. We must act on our thoughts! It is not sufficient to know what is pure and admirable, but we must also do what is pure and admirable. Our actions must complement our thinking; doctrine and practice belong together.

Such a life is a blessed life as Paul demonstrates when he writes: "And the God of peace will be with you." God will be with us then. As Psalm 1 says, the man who meditates on God's law day and night is blessed because the LORD watches over his way. It is not enough to be a Christian in name only. The Christian faith must permeate our thoughts and actions. Christ said, "Not everyone who says to Me 'Lord, Lord,' will enter the kingdom of heaven, but only he who does the will of My Father who is in heaven" (Mt 7:21). May these words of the Psalmist be a reality in our lives: "I meditate on Your precepts and consider Your ways. I delight in Your decrees; I will not neglect Your word" (Ps. 119:15, 16).

Read: James 2:14-26

Faith and Works Belong Together

In the same way, faith by itself, if it is not accompanied by action, is dead.

James 2:17

This blunt statement of James is intended to make people sit up and take notice. As James writes a little earlier, "What good is it, my brothers, if a man claims to have faith but has no deeds? Can such faith save him" (2:14)? The implicit answer to this question is clear: faith without deeds — dead faith — cannot save anyone!

James is writing about a situation in which someone is all talk but no action. People sometimes speak very piously, but their actions do not measure up. Sometimes people in the church say, "Oh, I believe!" but they live in a worldly way. Such talk is useless because James asks, "What good is it . . ." (2:14)? It is about as useful as when you say to a person without clothing and food that you wish him well, but you do nothing to supply him with his physical needs (2:15, 16). And then James concludes, "*In the same way*, faith by itself, if it is not accompanied by action, is dead." Just as all talk and no action will not help a distressed person, so all talk and no action will not help anyone who wants to be saved! Our talk must be complemented by our walk for the talk to have any meaning.

Actually, this so-called dead faith is no faith because faith is alive. When a person is alive, he moves around and acts; in the same way, when faith is alive and well, it manifests itself in actions (2:26). This is why the Apostle Paul speaks about ". . . faith expressing itself through love" (Gal 5:6).

James then introduces someone who presents a supposed counter-argument: "But someone will say, 'You have faith; I have deeds'" (2:18). According to this counter-argument, people have different emphases in life, but they all serve the LORD in their own way. Some people do not put their faith into practice while others do, but together they serve the LORD. In response, James issues a challenge: "Show me your faith without deeds, and I will show you my faith by what I do" (2:18). James is saying that it is impossible to *show* your faith, except by deeds. You can *say* that you believe, but that does not *show* it. James goes on to say that "God is one" (2:19; ESV), whereby he means that there is a wholeness about God by which God's words and deeds complement each other. The implication is that God also wants there to be a wholeness in our lives, by which our works complement our faith. Someone who claims to be a Christian cannot profess faith in God and live in an ungodly manner!

James uses Abraham and Rahab as examples of people who put faith into action. Abraham was even willing to sacrifice Isaac to the LORD because he believed that the LORD could raise the dead in order to fulfil His promise that from Isaac many descendants would come forth (Heb 11:17-19). "You see that his faith and his actions were working together, and his faith was made complete by what he did" (2:22). Likewise in the case of Rahab. Her faith in Israel's God was evident from the lodging and protection she offered the spies at great risk to herself (2:25).

Works flow from faith and are the evidence of faith. Throughout the New Testament, we read about works as the fruit of faith. Paul tells the Colossians about his prayer that they ". . . may live a life worthy of the Lord and may please Him in every way: bearing fruit in every good work, growing in the knowledge of God" (Col 1:10). And in his first letter to the Thessalonians, Paul writes: "We continually remember before our God and Father your work produced by faith . . ." (I Thess 1:3). The Lord Jesus Christ taught, "I am the vine; you are the branches. If a man remains in Me and I in him, he will bear much fruit . . ." (Jn 15:5). And Christ also said: "By their fruit you will recognize them . . . A good tree cannot bear bad fruit, and a bad tree cannot bear good fruit . . . Not everyone who says to Me, 'Lord, Lord,' will enter the kingdom of heaven, but only he who does the will of My Father who is in heaven" (Mt 7:16, 18, 21).

Therefore, the prayer of our lives should be: "Teach me Your way, O LORD, and I will walk in Your truth; give me an undivided heart, that I may fear Your Name" (Ps. 86:11).

Read: I Peter 1: 1-12

Our Certain and Glorious Inheritance

*Praise be to the God and Father of our Lord Jesus
Christ! In His great mercy He has given us new birth
into a living hope through the resurrection of Jesus
Christ from the dead, and into an inheritance that can
never perish, spoil or fade — kept in heaven for
you . . .*

I Peter 1:3, 4

The believers scattered throughout Asia Minor were disappointed. These Gentile Christians had joined the church with the enthusiasm of new believers, but they were frustrated by the consequences of being Christians. People began to ridicule them for no longer participating in an immoral lifestyle (I Pt 4:3, 4). In that situation, they were tempted to go the road of least resistance and fall back into their old way of life. Therefore, Peter warns them, "As obedient children, do not conform to the evil desires you had when you lived in ignorance" (I Pt 1:14). Is every generation of Christians not tempted to conform to the world? In this letter, Peter impresses upon us that the riches of the gospel are far greater than anything this world offers.

For this reason, Peter begins his letter by speaking so joyfully about our certain and glorious inheritance. A strong awareness of the hope of faith is the antidote against the temptation to live as the world. If it were not for God the Father's mercy, we would be without hope in the world and we would be trying to fill the void by various sensual pleasures. But the gospel offers something much better: God the Father sent His Son to pull us out of the mire of sin and misery and put us on the road to eternal salvation.

Foundational to the Christian hope is the resurrection of Jesus Christ from the dead because therein lies the *certainty* of our inheritance. After Christ paid the price for our sins on the cross, the Father raised Him from the dead as the evidence that Christ's redeeming work was truly finished. By dying in our place, Christ obtained eternal life for God's people, and He arose as the firstfruits of those who are dead (I Cor 15:20).

Thus the Father has given us new birth into a living hope. Our lives are revitalized because we have this living hope. We have a new lease on life, knowing that life has been redeemed from the bondage of sin and death. Christ has freed us from being held in slavery by fear of death because we have the hope of the resurrection (Heb 2:15). Peter calls this a *living hope*. It is not the kind of hope about which a person is unsure, but it is a certain hope and therefore a living hope. This hope may dominate all our thoughts, words, and actions; it causes us to live in a state of expectation. The Christian hope may and must influence all aspects of our lives and mould us into a people different than the world around us. That is why Peter goes on to write, "Therefore, prepare your minds for action; be self-controlled; set your hope fully on the grace to be given you when Jesus Christ is revealed" (I Pt 1:13). Precisely because we have the prospect of living in perfect fellowship with God on the new earth, we have every reason to resist the temptation to conform to the lifestyle of the world. We must look beyond the hardships we suffer as Christians and look to the certain inheritance.

And it is a *glorious* inheritance. Peter writes that it can never perish, spoil or fade. The hardships which Christians sometimes must endure for the sake of the gospel are only transient. In comparison with eternity, the grief we must sometimes suffer in all kinds of trials lasts only for a little while (1:6). Peter is hereby discouraging us from trading in the Christian life for short-term gain in this life. And Peter and the other apostles certainly knew what hardship was all about!

After all, whatever this world offers has no permanence. An illustrious career, lots of money, expensive cars, and exotic vacations will provide no lasting joy and happiness. How often do we buy something we really wanted, feel excited about it, but after a month or two we are already thinking of another wish? That's because our worldly possessions never really make or keep us happy. Moreover, all those things will slip out of our hands at the moment of death. And yet, we are often tempted to pursue such things at the expense of living as Christians. Peter's point is that we ought not to fix our hope on the things which the world offers us because they are fleeting. Rather, our living hope is the inheritance that can never perish, spoil, or fade — kept in heaven for us. The riches which God has prepared for us in Jesus Christ will not slip out of our hands but last into eternity!

As God's people, we live as strangers in the world (1:1). We are exiles in the world because this is not our homeland; our citizenship is in heaven (Php 3:20). Exiles often lose their possessions and status, and Christians often make many sacrifices for Christ's sake. But the gospel tells us that, as exiles in the world, we have an inheritance in heaven! "Praise be to the God and Father of our Lord Jesus Christ!"

Read: I Peter 1:13-2:3

Crave Pure Spiritual Milk!

*Like newborn babies, crave pure spiritual milk, so
that by it you may grow up in your salvation, now that
you have tasted that the Lord is good.*
I Peter 2:2, 3

The LORD has called us to His grace in Christ Jesus and
now wants us to walk in thankfulness before Him. He expects
from us a life of commitment and service to Him. Such a life of
service is not easy because we must contend with our sinful old
nature as well as opposition from the world (I Pt 1:13, 14; 4:4).
In such circumstances, Peter shows us the way to a committed
Christian life when he commands: "Crave pure spiritual milk!"

This pure spiritual milk is the Word of God. In the previous
chapter, Peter says that we have been born again ". . . through
the living and enduring word of God" (1:23). In fact, Peter may
be employing a play on words when he uses a term for "spiritual"
which sounds similar to the term for "Word." The Holy Spirit
uses the Word to regenerate us and also to nourish us in the
faith.

Peter commands us to crave the Word like newborn babies,
thereby expressing the intense desire believers must have for
the Word. It is to be a craving, just like babies crave milk. Babies
know what they need, and their heads always turn in that
direction. Like a baby reaches for mother, we must reach for the
Word. The milk of the Word is our lifeline! Peter's reference to
milk should not make us think that we can be satisfied with the
simple truths of God's Word and do not need solid food. Peter
simply uses the image of a baby craving milk, with the focus on
the craving.

Peter also specifies what we should crave because he speaks
about "*pure* spiritual milk." Again, there may be a play on words

because the word for "pure" is closely related to the word for "deceit" in 2:1. The Word of God is "without deceit" because it does not mislead us but shows us the way we must go. Moreover, it must be presented without deceit. We must crave the "unadulterated" Word of God, not a watered-down version. Our sinful nature would like to embrace a watered-down version because then we may not have to make any changes in our lives. Moreover, the world can tolerate Christians who conform to the practices of the world, and by embracing such a Christianity we would no longer be marginalized by society. Compromising certainly seems practical and easy. But Peter tells us to crave *pure* spiritual milk.

When faced with the pressures of our sinful old nature and the pressures of the world, we need to be nourished by the Word which shows us the grandeur of the gospel in contrast to what our sinful old nature and the world offer us. As Peter says, ". . . crave pure spiritual milk . . . now that you have tasted that the Lord is good." Also here, Peter may be using a play on words because the word for "goodness" sounds very similar to the Name "Christ." God's goodness toward us is revealed in Christ, who bore the punishment for our sins. Christ went the way of the cross because of our sins, and He arose as victor over death and the grave. The goodness of the Lord is that we have ". . . a living hope through the resurrection of Jesus Christ from the dead . . ." and ". . . an inheritance that can never perish, spoil or fade . . ." (I Pt 1:3, 4).

It is in this salvation that we must mature. Peter says, ". . . crave pure spiritual milk, so that by it you may grow up in your salvation . . ." In the original, the verb for "growing up" is in a form indicating that God is the One who gives the growth. It is as Paul writes, "I planted the seed, Apollos watered it, but God made it grow" (I Cor 3:6). The fact that God gives the growth does not take away from the purpose of the command because we must use the means in order that God may give the growth. Our responsibility is to attend the preaching of the Word faithfully and to read the Word regularly.

What does it mean to grow up in our salvation? It means that the Holy Spirit will impress upon us the height and depth of the gospel of salvation. It means that there will be spiritual growth in our lives. As a baby is nourished by milk and becomes stronger, so the believer will be nourished by the Word and become stronger in the faith. When we drink in the Word, we will know better how to live out of the Word in all aspects of life. Then we will also be more and more able to live lives of thankfulness to God expressed in commitment and service to Him. This will also be expressed in love and service to one another as members of Christ's church (1:22, 23; 2:1). This spiritual growth is a life-long process!

And then we will also be better able to resist the pressures of the sinful old nature and the pressures of the world. For, then we will more and more have our hearts set on the inheritance which Christ has obtained for us — the inheritance which can never perish, spoil, or fade (I Pt 1:4).

Crave pure spiritual milk!

Read: Ephesians 6:10-18

Be Alert!

*Be self-controlled and alert. Your enemy the devil
prowls around like a roaring lion looking for someone
to devour. Resist him, standing firm in the faith,
because you know that your brothers throughout the
world are undergoing the same kind of sufferings.*
I Peter 5:8, 9

Peter originally wrote this letter to believers scattered throughout Asia Minor, an area which we today call Turkey. He refers to his readers as ". . . strangers in the world . . ." (I Pt 1:1) — exiles in the world. These early Christians were not exiles in a literal sense but in a metaphorical sense. They were living where they had always lived, but now they were living there as strangers because they had received the gospel of Jesus Christ in faith. They were now different than before they were Christians, and they no longer fit in with those around them. To say it concisely: they were in the world but not of the world. For this reason, Peter writes, "Dear friends, I urge you, as aliens and strangers in the world, to abstain from sinful desires, which war against your soul" (I Pt 2:11). Understanding this about the first readers, we realize that we have the same status in the world.

Precisely because we are Christians, the devil prowls around looking for someone to devour. The devil seeks to devour us by making us lose sight of our exile in the world! The first readers had received the Word of salvation with joy, but they became disappointed with the cost of being a Christian. Since they no longer fit in with the people around them, they were subject to ridicule (I Pt 4:4). This they had not counted on, and they were surprised at their suffering (I Pt 4:12). It is easy to imagine that they were tempted to cave in and go along with the crowd. Therefore Peter writes: "As obedient children, do not conform to the evil desires you had when you lived in ignorance" (I Pt 1:14). They had to remember that they were strangers in the world! We too are easily tempted to forget about our status as exiles and to go along with the crowd. The devil tempts us to pursue the same entertainment as the world, to have the same friends, to use our money in the same way, and to have the same priorities in life. So easily we think that the cost of being a Christian is too high.

This is the work of the devil who is prowling around. Peter refers to the devil as our "enemy." The devil is antagonistic toward God's work in our lives and wants to destroy God's work in us. The devil wants to draw us to his side by making us lose sight of our special status as God's children who have been called out of this world to serve God. Like a lion picking off sheep from the flock, so the devil prowls around ready to pounce on God's children and carry them off as his prey.

That is why Peter says, "Be self-controlled and alert." We must reckon with the devil, realizing that his existence is very real and has serious implications for us. We must be self-controlled, that is, of clear mind and seeing things in proper perspective. We must be alert, that is, always on our guard and watchful. In other words, we must not be easily impressed and drawn in by the people and things around us but have discerning, spiritual eyes that analyze the situation properly. Our eyes must be wide open, for the very reason that the devil is trying to make us lose sight of our exile.

When we recognize the devil, we are to resist the devil. We are to resist the devil by using the Word of God, which is the sword of the Spirit (Eph 6:17). Recall that when the Lord Jesus Christ was tempted by the devil in the desert He used the Word of God to resist the advances of the devil (Mt 4:1-11). And the devil left Christ (Mt 4:11)!

So often a Christian thinks that he is the only one engaged in this struggle against the devil. In fact, one of the devil's tricks is to make a person feel all alone, because such a feeling makes the struggle seem all the more burdensome. An isolated person more easily falls victim to the devil. But Peter reminds us that we are not alone, when he writes: ". . . because you know that your brothers throughout the world are undergoing the same kind of sufferings." Rather than feeling all alone in the struggle of faith, we may remind ourselves that we are part of the catholic church throughout the world. The personal difficulties we have in the struggle of faith are experienced by many Christians throughout the world. The unity of the faith unites us with them as we together look to Jesus Christ.

God's Word teaches that, although the devil prowls around like a roaring lion, he is a defeated enemy. The victory belongs to Christ because Christ defeated the devil by His death and resurrection. The Revelation to John includes a comforting contrast to the scenario in Peter's first letter when it says, "See, the Lion of the tribe of Judah, the Root of David, has triumphed" (Rev 5:5).

Therefore, be alert and resist the devil, knowing that the victory belongs to Jesus Christ!

Read: I John 2:18-27

See to it That What You Heard Remains in You!

See that what you have heard from the beginning remains in you. If it does, you also will remain in the Son and in the Father. And this is what He promised us — even eternal life.

I John 2:24, 25

The believers to whom John initially wrote this letter were faced with a serious doctrinal error: some people denied that Jesus is the Christ, the Son of God who came in the flesh (2:22; I Jn 4:2, 3, 15). This heresy undermined the entire Christian gospel and touched the foundation of the Christian church. After all, when Peter exclaimed in the presence of Jesus, "You are the Christ, the Son of the living God" (Mt 16:16), the Lord Jesus said to Peter, ". . . on this rock I will build My church . . ." (Mt 16:16). On this apostolic witness, Jesus Christ would build His church as the disciples became apostles sent out to proclaim the gospel of salvation through faith in Him.

Is it any different today? There are many so-called Christians who teach heresy about the person of Christ by claiming that Jesus was only a noble man who taught words of great wisdom and denying that Jesus is the Christ, the Son of the living God. We too must hear the Apostle John's exhortation. It is an urgent matter. John even stresses the contrast between believers and false teachers by beginning verse 24 very emphatically in the original: *You* see to it that what you have heard from the beginning remains in you!

John's exhortation may sound a little strange to Reformed ears because John tells *us* to see to it that what we heard from the beginning remains in us. Don't we usually say that God does that? Is the perseverance of the saints not God's work? Yes, it is God's work, but we should not create false dilemmas, because God involves us in the execution of his work. Nowhere does Scripture teach that because faith is God's work in us all we must do is sit with folded arms, waiting for God to do His work. John's exhortation clearly counters such thinking and teaches that we have our responsibility as God preserves us in the faith. Faith is the work of the Holy Spirit, but the Spirit uses the Word to create and strengthen faith. Therefore, we must be busy with the Word!

We have the complete gospel about Jesus Christ, and we do not need anyone to teach us something different from that gospel (2:27). Moreover, we have the anointing of the Holy Spirit enabling us to understand God's truth (2:20). Our responsibility is to work with what God has given us. We must regularly attend the preaching of God's Word and study God's Word personally. This is what John has in mind with his exhortation.

This is an urgent matter because it is so easy to succumb to false teaching which undermines the gospel in some way. Likewise, it is so easy to be enticed by the pleasures of the world, with the result that we turn our backs on the gospel of Christ. We must see to it that we stay focussed on Jesus Christ crucified and risen, the Saviour from sin and death.

God also gives a promise. John says that if what we heard from the beginning remains in us, we also will remain in the Son and in the Father. Notice the parallel in what John says: the Word must remain in us for us to remain in the Son and in the Father. John even emphasizes the parallel: if the Word remains in you, *also* you will remain in God. Fellowship with God is only possible when the Word dwells in us. In order to walk with God and experience His nearness, we must walk close to the Word.

By believing the Word we remain in the Son and in the Father! God's promise is that if we believe in Jesus Christ, we have fellowship with Him. As Christ Himself said, "I am the way and the truth and the life. No one comes to the Father except through Me" (Jn 14:6). John says, "No one who denies the Son has the Father; whoever acknowledges the Son has the Father also" (2:23).

And when we have fellowship with God, we have salvation. John continues by saying: "And this is what He promised us — even eternal life." That is how high the stakes are! John repeats it later in his letter when he writes, "And this is the testimony: God has given us eternal life, and this life is in His Son. He who has the Son has life; he who does not have the Son of God does not have life" (I Jn 5:11, 12).

Therefore, see to it that what you heard remains in you!

Read: I John 4:7-21

Love One Another

Dear friends, since God so loved us, we also ought to love one another.

I John 4:11

Every time we celebrate the Lord's Supper, we are reminded of this text. The *Form for the Celebration of the Lord's Supper*, as historically used by the Reformed Churches, refers to this text when it states that "For the sake of Christ, who so exceedingly loved us, we shall now love one another, and shall show this to one another not just in words but also in deeds." Christ's love toward us — and God the Father's love toward us — is the example for our love toward our brothers and sisters. As John writes, ". . . since God so loved us, we also ought to love one another." It is very fitting that the *Form* ties in with this because at the Lord's Supper we *together* celebrate our fellowship with the Saviour, and therefore a sense of *togetherness* should prevail among the congregation — a togetherness which finds expression in love for one another in words and deeds.

The text summarizes the immediately preceding verses. John writes: ". . . since God *so* loved us . . ." With that little word "so" John summarizes what he has written in the immediately preceding verses. What was the nature of God's love, and how did God manifest His love?

We did not love God, but God loved us (4:10). We were completely detestable in the sight of God because of our sin but God, of His own goodness and sovereign good pleasure, loved us and sent His Son as the atoning sacrifice for our sins. John describes the Son as God's "one and only Son" (4:9) in order to emphasize the sacrifice which God made to arrive at our redemption. In order that we might live through Christ, God sent His one and only Son "into the world" (4:9). This means that God sent His Son into a corrupt place, thereby leading him into a state of humiliation. God did all this so that His Son could atone for our sins and so that we might live through Him. By His suffering and death on the cross, our Lord Jesus Christ freed us from eternal death and secured for us eternal life. John writes: This is love!

John says: ". . . since God so loved us, we also ought to love one another." Thus, the grand statements about God's love, summarized by that short phrase ". . . God so loved us . . . ," are followed by a very practical exhortation. And John even emphasizes it by addressing us very literally as *beloved* (translated as *dear friends* in the NIV). We are the beloved of God since God has so loved us, and now we also ought to love one another. The beloved of God ought to love one another. When John says that we *ought* to love one another, he is not suggesting that it is optional. John means that we are *obligated* to love one another.

This is a very simple truth, and we all know it. Nothing new here. But it goes against our old sinful nature, and therefore we must be reminded of it. This love does not come from within us, but it is worked in us from above. A few verses before the text, John speaks about loving in connection with being "born of God" (4:7). Love means self-sacrifice, just as the Father sacrificed His one and only Son, and this is not something we do naturally. God works it *in* our lives and, through the working of the Holy Spirit, we must work it *out* in our lives. Hence the exhortation in the text. God wants to see this self-sacrificial love in our lives as we relate to one another. And this love of which the text speaks recurs throughout this letter. In 3:16, John writes, "This is how we know what love is: Jesus Christ laid down His life for us. And we ought to lay down our lives for our brothers." At the end of chapter 4, John writes, "We love because He first loved us" (4:19).

Love is an integral part of the communion of saints. We have communion with Christ, and we have communion with one another through Christ. This is why the Heidelberg Catechism says that in the church ". . . everyone is duty-bound to use his gifts readily and cheerfully for the benefit and well-being of the other members" (Lord's Day 21 Q&A 55). As we sit at the Lord's Supper table, we are reminded of the bond which ties all of us together. We are one in Christ, whom the Father sent into this world to atone for our sins. God's love for us must be reflected in our love for one another. As members of one body, we must display true brotherly love.

Show Christian love to the spiritually weak, the troubled, the bereaved, the lonely, and the sick within the congregation. Overcome personal conflict by focussing on Christian love. Seek the good for one another (I Thess 5:15). Count the other more worthy than yourself (Php 2:3). That takes self-sacrifice. That is love.

To Love God Means to Obey God

This is love for God: to obey His commands.
I John 5:3a

We usually associate love with a feeling. When we love someone, we have a strong feeling for that person. When we love God, we . . . yes, we what? Is love for God some kind of feeling? What kind of feeling? No doubt love for God does involve feelings since love for God is closely connected with the thankfulness and joy that we ought to experience in His service. In the *Book of Praise's* rhymed version of Psalm 116:1, we sing: "I love the LORD, the fount of life and grace . . ." The Psalmist then thankfully and joyfully expresses how the LORD rescued him from dire circumstances. This thankfulness and joy cause him to exclaim that he loves the LORD, and at the end of the Psalm he exclaims, "Praise the LORD" (Ps. 116:19). But there is more to the Psalmist's love than feelings. Twice the Psalmist says, "I will fulfil my vows to the LORD in the presence of all His people (Ps 116:14, 18). In other words, *obedience* also characterizes the Psalmist's love for God! Taking the whole of Scripture into account, one can say that obedience has the upperhand when it comes to a definition of loving God.

John writes, "This is love for God: to obey His commands." That is a very clear statement. Love for God is characterized by obedience; to love God means to obey God. There is nothing vague or indefinite about that.

In the verse preceding the text, John mentions in one breath loving God and carrying out His commands, and in the text he focusses on this. The connection is very clear in the original because there is the little connecting word "for": "*For* this is love for God . . ." It is as if John is saying that we heard correctly in verse 2 that love for God and carrying out His commandments go together.

It is important for us to hear this. Sometimes we say that we love the LORD, but we do not show it in our deeds. We say that we are thankful to the LORD for the redeeming work of Jesus Christ, but it does not show much in our lives. This love for God seems to be little more than a feeling that wells up in us from time to time. We know that we are God's covenant children but do not always live according to God's standards. Sometimes we ignore God's commandments and live as we please for extended periods. Earlier in this letter, John writes that if we walk in darkness we do not have fellowship with God (I Jn 1:6), and John goes on to say, "We know that we have come to know Him if we obey His commands" (I Jn 2:3). We can say over and over again that we love God, but John says, "This is love for God: to obey his commands." If our actions belie our words, our words mean nothing!

In this letter, John writes much about God sending His Son in the flesh to be our Saviour. In 5:11, John says, "And this is the testimony: God has given us eternal life, and this life is in His Son." As John writes in his gospel, God so *loved* the world that He gave His only Son (Jn 3:16). God's love led to the *deed* of giving His Son. God did not rest with just having a fuzzy, warm feeling toward us. God's love led to action, and so too must ours. John writes in this letter that "We love because He first loved us" (I Jn 4:19). Our love for God must be evident in deeds of obedience, that is, in living according to God's commands in the things of daily life.

The clear implication of the text is that if we do not obey God's commands by persisting in sin, we do not love God! This is strong language, but it is what the text teaches. It should shake us up, if we are willfully not living according to God's commandments. And it should lead to repentance.

Have You Forsaken Your First Love?

Yet I hold this against you: You have forsaken your first love.

Revelation 2:4

This is the first of the seven letters to the seven churches in Asia Minor. Each of the seven churches received all seven messages because John was told to send the entire revelation to the seven churches (Rev 1:11). Moreover, each of the seven messages includes the refrain, "He who has an ear, let him hear what the Spirit says to *the churches.*" Furthermore, there were more than seven churches at the time when John wrote, but these seven churches were representative of them all because seven is the number of fullness. Since these messages are intended for the fullness of Christ's church, they are also valid for us today.

This first message is written to "... *the angel* of the church in Ephesus ..." (2:1). This can hardly refer to what we normally consider an angel because Christ told John to *send* the revelation to the seven churches. How does one send a letter to an angel? The word *angel* simply means *messenger*, and so this message was written to the minister of the church at Ephesus. The minister proclaims God's message to the congregation by explaining God's Word in preaching and teaching. He addresses the congregation on behalf of Christ, who holds the ministers in His right hand and walks among the churches (2:1; cf. Rev 1:20).

Christ begins this message with words of praise about Ephesus' concern for doctrinal purity. When the Apostle Paul spoke his words of farewell to the Ephesian elders, he warned them that savage wolves would come in among the flock, distorting the truth and seeking to attract disciples. Paul had told them to be on their guard (Acts 20:29-31). The church at Ephesus had been on its guard because Christ says, "I know your deeds, your hard work and your perseverance. I know that you cannot tolerate wicked men, that you have tested those who claim to be apostles but are not, and have found them false" (2:2). In defending the truth of the gospel, the Ephesians had even endured hardships for Christ's sake and had not grown weary (2:3). At the time John wrote, they were still defending the Christian doctrine over against detractors (2:6).

But something was lacking because Christ says, "Yet I hold this against you: You have forsaken your first love." The Ephesians were still fighting for doctrinal purity, but they were doing so without their first love. When the Ephesians were new believers, they served God with love and delight, but after a while their service degenerated into doing all the right things out of routine. Christ does not say that they had *no love* for God's service anymore, but that their *first love* was gone. To a certain extent, their service was a matter of going through the motions, and God held this against them.

How easily we forsake our first love! And this impacts every aspect of our lives as Christians. Our participation in church activities decreases because we consider other activities more appealing. Our interest in studying the Bible wanes because we deem other pursuits more stimulating. Our financial support for the church decreases because we would rather spend money on ourselves. Our entertainment becomes more worldly because we are less concerned about what God thinks about our lifestyle. This text makes us reflect on whether we personally, the congregation of which we are members, and the federation of churches to which we belong are being described in this message to Ephesus. Have we forsaken our first love?

Jesus Christ, the Head of the church, wants our hearts. If the words of this text are applicable in our situation, we must heed the warning: "Remember the height from which you have fallen! Repent and do the things you did at first. If you do not repent, I will come to you and remove your lampstand from its place" (2:5). The removal of the lampstand is a serious threat because it means that the church at Ephesus would cease to exist.

The light of God's Word would be snuffed out there. This would not necessarily happen overnight but could be a gradual development resulting in the disappearance of the church. It would hit them even at their present strong point because if the first love for God is gone, the love for the truth of God's Word also begins to languish. A development occurs in which people first do not know the truth through lack of study, then people do not want to know the truth anymore, and finally people distort the truth.

If the text portrays our situation, we do well to hear what the Spirit says to the churches (2:7) because otherwise we could lose our love for God entirely, with terrible eternal consequences. Christ says, "To him who overcomes, I will give the right to eat from the tree of life, which is in the paradise of God" (2:7). The present tense of the word "overcome" could even indicate that it is a daily struggle for believers to maintain their first love for God. Every day we must overcome the things that draw us away from that first love. "He who has an ear, let him hear what the Spirit says to the churches" (2:7).

The Dort Study Bible

An English translation of the Annotations to the Dutch Staten Bijbel of 1637 in accordance with a decree of the Synod of Dort 1618-1619

Rev. Jerome Julien in *The Outlook*: This is a wonderful addition to a home, church, school, or minister's library . . . Originally, these notes were commissioned by the Great Synod of Dort, 1618-1619, along with the Staten Bijbel, a completely new translation of Scripture. In a very real sense, this is probably the earliest study Bible ever produced. We might say of it that it is a short commentary on the Bible.

This volume, the first of what is planned, D.V., to be a republication of the whole set of annotations, contains an historical sketch — written most likely by Theodore Haak, and other documents from the 1637 Dutch edition. There is also an account of a gold coin produced by the States General of the United Netherlands commemorating the Synod. This coin is also stamped in gold on the front and back covers. (It *must* be added that the binding is beautiful!) Inside the front and back covers are reprinted the title pages of the Dutch Staten Bijbel and the English translation by Haak, dated 1657.

The notes are preceded by an introduction to each Bible book, and a summary at the head of each chapter. While the notes on Genesis are much more detailed due to the nature of the content, many insights are found on all the pages. These notes might not be what you would read in a commentary published today, but they give concise explanations of the verses. Regularly, they give cross references to other Biblical passages which shed further light on what God says in the text. Also, these notes give a historic-redemptive understanding of the Bible history. Ministers, as well as Bible students, will find helpful information here, as well as ideas to develop.

For those who might be interested, the position on creation days is "that night and day . . . made up one natural day together . . . comprehending twenty-four hours" (see Genesis 1:5). Further, the Book of Genesis lays open God's "everlasting covenant." The note on Genesis 17:7 states that it is "Everlasting for all believers in Christ . . ." This subject is discussed at great length in the appropriate places.

Of what value is this new, but very old set of notes? Some scholars might look with disdain on a republication of these notes. Yet, historically they have value because we can read in English what our fathers at Dort taught and believed concerning Biblical teachings other than those well explained in the Canons of Dort. It is foolhardy to cut ourselves off from our heritage, as so many wish to do today. Now, what has been readily available in the Dutch language for the last 350 years, is in a newly translated and typeset English edition for our reading and spiritual benefit.

Further, this volume has a practical value. For those who still attend church society meetings, or for those involved in Bible studies, here is a concise and helpful Reformed commentary. Its format allows it to be on the table with our Bibles, Psalters, and notes.

This is an ambitious project which Inheritance has undertaken. We must be grateful for their dedicated work. It is the hope of this reviewer that the day will come, beginning now, when this set will not only be displayed in many, many homes, but also well worn through use. In this day of seemingly shrinking interest in the Reformed Faith we and our children must be grounded in God's Truth!

Vol. 1 Genesis and Exodus	ISBN 1-894666-51-8	Can.$24.95 U.S.$21.90
Vol. 2 Leviticus - Deuteronomy	ISBN 1-894666-52-6	Can.$24.95 U.S.$21.90
Vol. 3 Joshua - 2 Samuel	ISBN 1-894666-53-4	Can.$24.95 U.S.$21.90

Sample Pages of *The Dort Study Bible*

In a time of much confusion and debate about reliable manuscripts of God's Word, as well as the proper place of God's Church, Covenant, and the Christ-centeredness of the whole Bible, there is an urgent need to reach back to one of the best and possibly only ecclesiastical translation of the Bible ever made. Even though the States General of the United Netherlands authorized this translation, it did so upon a decree of the famous Synod of Dort (1618-1619). The high value of this translation and its annotations — also written by the translators, who were among the best theologians of the early seventeenth century — is evident in the example below. The translators were not bothered by publishers who wanted to have as big a market as possible and so make compromises to avoid controversies — as is the case so much today — but seriously looked at what God revealed in His Word and stuck faithfully to the text. Their humbleness in often not being sure of what the text really means is evident throughout the annotations, nevertheless they have given a faithful translation of these texts. There is no better tool for the unity of God's church today then abiding by a reliable Bible translation and explanation. Since this English translation is not a direct translation of the original texts, it would not be suitable as a current ecclesiastical translation, but nevertheless it may be one of the best tools to come to a new ecclesiastical translation. In the meantime it is a number one tool for personal and group Bible study for those who cannot read the original languages.
— Roelof A. Janssen, editor and publisher.

2 Samuel 23

The last words of David, in which he testifies of his calling from God to the royal and prophetical office, v. 1. He prophesies of the Messiah Jesus Christ, and the blessed salvation under His reign, with the acknowledgment of the faults of his house, and a confession of his confidence in God's everlasting covenant of grace, v. 3. He announces everlasting destruction to the ungodly, v. 6. A history of David's heroes and their courage, v. 8.

1. Moreover, these are the last words[1] of David. David the son of Jesse says, and the man who was raised up on high, the anointed[2] of the God of Jacob, and pleasant *in* Psalms[3] of Israel, says:

[1] Before his death, according to the example of Jacob in Gen. 49, and of Moses in Deut. 32 & 33.

[2] Lifted up from low conditions and anointed as king over the people of God.

[3] Which he wrote for the church of God by the inspiration of the Holy Spirit.

2. "The Spirit of the LORD has spoken through me, and His word has been upon my tongue. 3. "The God of Israel has said, the Rock[4] of Israel has spoken to me:[5] *"There shall be* a Ruler over the people, a righteous *Person,*[6] a Ruler *in the* fear of God.[7]

[4] As also in 2 Sam. 22:2. Compare 1 Cor. 10:4.

[5] Or, *of me*; meaning that David here relates the prophecies which God had given him concerning himself, his kingdom, and his house, partly to David himself, partly to the prophets, Samuel, Nathan, etc.

[6] See Is. 53:11; Jer. 23:5, 6; 33:15, 16; Zech. 9:9 and its annotations.

[7] Compare Is. 11:2, 3. Understand by this Ruler our eternal spiritual King and Lord Jesus Christ, whose type David (as also Solomon) was, and of whom God had revealed to him that He should proceed from his seed, (according to the flesh). See Ps. 2:8; 72:8; Jer. 30:21; Micah 5:2. Others understand it as a description of the virtues and duties of rulers or governors, applying to it also the following comparison in 2 Sam. 23:4, as by this the graciousness and usefulness of such rulers as David and Solomon is meant, though lacking in much.

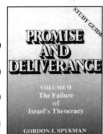
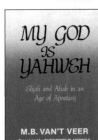

The Self-Justification of God in the Life of Job
by Kornelis Sietsma

Christine Farenhorst in *Christian Renewal*: While reading these sermons both my husband and myself became convinced of the fact that Rev. Sietsma was a compassionate and caring shepherd. His concern for and knowledge of the sheep in his care is obvious. The message of the all-powerful providential hand of God, so necessary for our own time, is conveyed.

Subject: Book of Job **Age: 16-99**
ISBN0-921100-24-8 **Can.$10.95 U.S.$8.90**

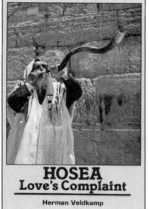

Hosea: Love's Complaint
by Herman Veldkamp

Jealousy, adultery, pain — these are the themes that dominate the prophecy of Hosea. Against the background of his deteriorating marriage Hosea addresses an urgent message to all of God's people begging them to listen to the complaint raised by the Lord's wounded love. Herman Veldkamp skilfully illuminates the prophet's hard hitting accusations.

Ideal for Bible Study societies. **(Six or more copies: 15% discount)**

Subject: Book of Hosea **Age: 16-99**
ISBN 0-88815-031-8 **Can.$9.95 U.S.$8.90**

The Farmer from Tekoa (Amos)
by Herman Veldkamp

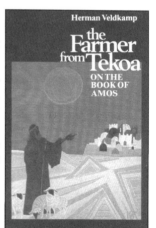

Written in a very attractive style, this commentary [on the book of Amos] can be enjoyed by young people and adults.
— *The Presbyterian Journal*

Not only ministers, teachers, and students but indeed every serious-minded reader will find in this book tremendous helpful, brilliantly beautiful guidelines to understanding the prophetic messages of Amos.
— *The Banner*

Subject: Book of Amos **Age: 16-99**
ISBN 0-88815-000-8 **Can.$9.95 U.S.$8.90**

Is the Bible a Jigsaw Puzzle . . .
by T. Boersma

An Evaluation of Hal Lindsey's Writings. Is Lindsey's "jigsaw puzzle" approach the proper way to read Scripture? Was the Bible written to foretell the events of our decade?

Subject: Book of Revelation **Age: 16-99**
ISBN 0-88815-019-9 **Can.$7.95 U.S.$6.90**

Hal Lindsey and Biblical Prophecy by C. Van der Waal

Hal Lindsey uses Biblical prophecy to open a supermarket, writes the author, a supermarket in which he sells inside information about the near future, especially World War III. The source of his information are the books of Daniel, Revelation, Ezekiel, and Matthew 24. Come, buy and read! Dr. Van der Waal not only analyzes Lindsey's weaknesses and mistakes, he also lays down basic guidelines for reading Biblical prophecy - especially the book of Revelation.

Subject: Revelation   **Age: 16-99**
ISBN 0-921100-31-0   **Can.$9.95 U.S.$8.90**

What the Spirit Says to the Churches by Jerome M. Julien

Jelle Tuininga in *Christian Renewal*: The sermons are easy to read and to understand. . . the book is recommended, and would make a welcome gift.

Subject: Revelation 2 & 3   **Age: 12-99**
ISBN 0-921100-76-0   **Can.$9.95 U.S.$8.90**

Annotations to the Heidelberg Catechism by J. Van Bruggen

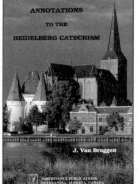

John A. Hawthorne in *Reformed Theological Journal*: . . . The individual Christian would find it a constructive way to employ part of the Sabbath day by working through the lesson that is set for each Lord's Day. No one can study this volume without increasing his knowledge of truth and being made to worship and adore the God of all grace. This book will help every minister in the instruction of his people, both young and not so young, every parent in the task of catechizing and is commended to every Christian for personal study.

Subject: Catechism   **Age: 13-99**
ISBN 0-921100-33-7   **Can.$15.95 U.S.$13.90**

Before the Face of God by Louis Praamsma

A Study of the Heidelberg Catechism in two workbooks for catechism students.

Subject: Catechism   **Age: 10-99**
Lords Day 1-24 ISBN 0-88815-056-3   **Can.$11.95 U.S.$9.90**
Lords Day 25-52 ISBN 0-88815-057-1   **Can.$11.95 U.S.$9.90**

The Church Says Amen by J. Van Bruggen An Exposition of the Belgic Confession

We need to stand on the shoulders of those who have gone before us, to learn how they applied God's promises in the grit and grime of life's struggles . . .
— from the *Preface* by C. Bouwman

W.L. Bredenhof in *Clarion*: This would be an excellent book for the use of study societies, for individual refreshment on the doctrines of the church, or as a textbook for preconfession or adult education.

Subject: Belgic Confession   **Age: 13-99**
ISBN 0-921100-17-5   **Can.$15.95 U.S.$13.90**

The Belgic Confession and its Biblical Basis
by Lepusculus Vallensis

The Belgic Confession is a Reformed Confession, dating from the 16th Century, written by Guido de Brès, a preacher in the Reformed Churches of The Netherlands. The great synod of Dort in 1618-19 adopted this Confession as one of the doctrinal standards of the Reformed Churches, to which all office-bearers of the Churches were (and still are) to subscribe. This book provides and explains the Scriptural proof texts for the Belgic Confession by using the marginal notes of the Dutch *Staten Bijbel*. The *Staten Bijbel* is a Dutch translation of the Bible, by order of the States General of the United Netherlands, in accordance with a decree of the Synod of Dort. It was first published in 1637 and included 'new explanations of difficult passages and annotations to comparative texts.'

Subject: Creeds   **Age: 15-99**
ISBN 0-921100-41-8   **Can.$17.95 U.S.$15.90**

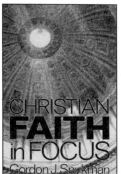

Christian Faith in Focus
by Gordon Spykman

This book is designed to serve the Christian Community as a study guide for personal enrichment and group discussions. Each of the thirty-two chapters is introduced by a pertinent Scripture passage, followed by brief explanations, leading up to questions which act as pump-primers for a free exchange of ideas.

Subject: Theology / Chr. Life   **Age: 16-99**
ISBN 0-88815-053-9   **Can.$9.95 U.S.$8.90**

The Church: Its Unity in Confession and History
by G. Van Rongen

"The planet on which we live is becoming smaller and smaller. It seems as if it is no longer true that the East is far from the West. Distances are shrinking. At the same time, our world of interest is becoming larger and larger. What is happening on the other side of the globe can be watched as it happens.

"In the field of church life, too, this process of shrinkage and expansion is going on. These modern times have brought us into contact with other churches which we had hardly ever heard of a few decades ago. After the war, our immigrant churches went through a period in which we settled into a new country and had to build up our church life from scratch. Now, however, we are able to have closer contact with our ecclesiastical environment and have discovered some of these churches.

This is what eighty-year-old Rev. G. Van Rongen writes in the Prologue of his book, which deals with what we believe concerning the Church of our Lord Jesus Christ. Rev. Van Rongen has spent the major part of his life pastoring and shepherding God's people in Reformed Churches in The Netherlands, the U.S.A., and Australia. Throughout this book and many of his other writings, it is clear that it is a great joy for him to serve his God and Saviour, as well as God's covenant community, the Church, by following in the footsteps of one of his earthly mentors, Dr. Klaas Schilder. Like Dr. Schilder, he has laboured in obedience to the prayer of the Lord Jesus Christ in John 17: "That they all may be one!"

Subject: History / Doctrine   **Age: 13-99**
ISBN 0-921100-90-6   **Can.$14.95 U.S.$12.90**

Our Reformed Church Service Book by G. Van Rongen

The author deals with the history of the *Book of Praise, Anglo-Genevan Psalter* and with the history of Reformed Psalters and liturgies from the early church till today.

Subject: Liturgy / Psalter   Age: 16-99
ISBN 0-921100-52-3   Can.$15.95 U.S.$13.90

A Sign of Faithfulness by H. Westerink

H. Westerink's book on Baptism is a jewel. One seldom comes across a book that simultaneously matches such simplicity to profundity, and vice versa. The author excels at clarifying the marvellous continuity (and discontinuity) between the old and new covenant with respect to the question of baptism — infant baptism in particular.
— J. Mark Beach

Subject: Covenant / Baptism   Age: 12-99
ISBN 0-921100-00-0   Can.$9.95 U.S.$8.90

John Calvin: Genius of Geneva
by Lawrence Penning
A Popular Account of the Life and Times of John Calvin

Penning shows the Life of Calvin against the turbulence, religious unrest, and intellectual ferment of the times, when Europe stormed with Reformation and Counter Reformation, and traces the incredible full life and work of the man who was not only the greatest of the of the sixteenth century Reformers, but who was the greatest man of his age. Here we see too, the man Calvin: a man of infinite tenderness as well as of great temper; one who despised money for himself, but who thought it very important when counseling a friend entertaining thoughts of marriage.

Time: 1509-1564   Age:15-99
ISBN 1-894666-77-1   Can.$19.95 U.S.$16.90

A Theatre in Dachau by Hermanus Knoop

In the concentration camp of Dachau the God of all grace did wonders of grace by His Word and Spirit every day. Oh, it was indeed a dreadful time for me that I spent there, and yet it is not at all a hollow phrase when I say that I would for no amount of money have missed this time of my life, since it was so unspeakably rich in grace. I saw God there. The LORD was in this place. It was a house of God and a gate of heaven.

Time: 1940-1943   Age: 14-99
ISBN 0-921100-20-5   Can.$14.95 U.S.$12.90

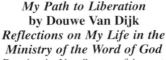

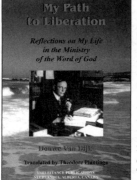

My Path to Liberation
by Douwe Van Dijk
Reflections on My Life in the Ministry of the Word of God

J. Bruning in *Una Sancta* of August 7, 2004: . . . In short, Rev van Dijk provides you with a realistic picture of the Church and its struggles, and encouragement to deal with current issues in a Scriptural and Church orderly manner. . . . I learned much from this book. Although written in a personal and easy style, it is a treasure for (future) office bearers and very educational for all who love the church. From time to time we hear the phrase "we have a rich Reformed heritage". This book definitely conveys some aspects of this heritage and will enrich you; it will also arm you.

Time: 1890-1960   Age: 16-99
ISBN 0-921100-26-4   Can.$19.95 U.S.$16.90

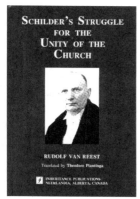

Schilder's Struggle for the Unity of the Church by Rudolf Van Reest

Klaas Schilder is remembered both for his courageous stand in opposition to Nazism, which led to his imprisonment three months after the Nazis overran The Netherlands in 1940, and for his role in the Church struggle in The Netherlands, which culminated in 1944 with the suspension of scores of office-bearers and the formation of the liberated Reformed Churches.

Thomas Vanden Heuvel in *The Outlook*: I strongly recommend this book for everyone interested in the preservation of and propagation of the Reformed faith.

Time: 1890-1952   **Age: 16-99**
ISBN 1-894666-79-8   **Can.\$19.95 U.S.\$17.90**

The Idea of Office by K. Sietsma

Henry Vander Kam in *Mid-America Journal of Theology*: The importance of this book is far greater than its small size . . . The author also deals with the office of all believers. He does so in the sense in which the Bible instructs us in this matter and as it was emphasized again by the reformers.

Subject: Christian Living   **Age: 15-99**
ISBN 0-88815-065-2   **Can.\$6.95 U.S.\$5.90**

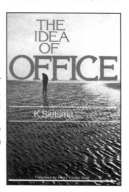

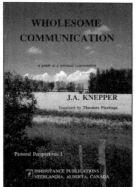

Wholesome Communication by J.A. Knepper
A Guide to a Spiritual Conversation

K.V. Warren in *Vox Reformata*: Here is plenty of practical and down to earth advice as regards the ins and outs of conversation in general: non-verbal communications and its importance, posture, value judgments, leading and structuring a conversation, etc.

G. Duncan Lowe in Covenanter Witness: This book deserves to be read throughout the Church. It is a manual of practical godliness within a clearly important area, and it is written by a man of experience and sensitivity who continually reflects upon God's Word.

Subject: Pastoral Care
ISBN 0-921100-13-2   **Can.\$9.95 U.S.\$8.90**

New . . .
New . . .

And They Sing A New Song by C. Van der Waal
About Psalms and Hymns

Reformed Churches have sung the Psalms for centuries. But what about the place of hymns in the worship services? Van der Waal shows from Holy Scripture and history what criteria churches should use for the Song of the Church. A must read for everyone who loves the Church of Christ and desires to do His will also in singing to the glory of His Name.

Subject: Psalms and Hymns   **Age: 14-99**
ISBN 978-1-894666-42-8   **Can.\$7.95 U.S.\$7.95**

Music Books & Compact Discs on the Genevan Psalms

The Genevan Psalms in Harmony
by Claude Goudimel

This book is ideal for churches, organists, choirs, and Christian families. Approximately 370 4-part settings of the Psalms. The melody is both in a Soprano and a Tenor setting, and all the stanzas of the Psalms from the *Book of Praise* are included.
ISBN 1-894666-66-6   Can.\$ 59.95 U.S.\$ 49.90
(15% discount for 6 or more copies!)

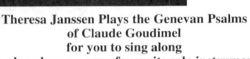

Theresa Janssen Plays the Genevan Psalms of Claude Goudimel
for you to sing along
(or play along on your favourite solo instrument)

An ideal set of 4 Compact Discs for those who want to learn to sing the Genevan Psalms by heart. Each of the 150 Psalms is played twice, once with the melody in the Soprano and once with the melody in the Tenor. The organ registrations (of the organs at West End Christian Reformed Church, Robertson-Wesley United Church, and Grace Lutheran Church in Edmonton, Alberta) used for each of the Psalms are available at **http://www.telusplanet.net/public/inhpubl/Goudimel.htm** which can be of great help for (young) organists.
4 Compact Discs CMR 109-112   **Can.\$ 40.00 U.S.\$34.00**

Great is the Lord! Him Greatly Laud
The Odé Ensemble Sings Anglo-Genevan Psalms of Claude Goudimel
Annelize Viljoen, soprano;
Helga Schabort & Philna Badenhorst, altos;
Antonie Fourie, tenor; Eric Kayayan, bass.
(The sheet music of this C.D. is published in *The Genevan Psalms in Harmony* by Claude Goudimel.)
Psalm 65:1 & 6; Psalm 38:1 & 10; Psalm 9:1 & 6; Psalm 28:1 & 5; Psalm 13:1 & 3; Psalm 43:1 & 5; Psalm 45:1 & 6; Psalm 37:1 & 5; Psalm 54:1 & 3; Psalm 32:1 & 5; Psalm 2:1 & 4; Psalm 40:1 & 7; Psalm 46:1 & 5; Psalm 62:1 & 6; Psalm 53:1 & 5; Psalm 17:1 & 5; Psalm 50:1 & 11; Psalm 34:1 & 7; Psalm 11:1 & 2; Psalm 41:1 & 4; Psalm 57:1 & 5; Psalm 59:1 & 8; Psalm 10:1 & 7; Psalm 26:1 & 7; Psalm 33:1 & 6; Psalm 48:1 & 4.
Compact Disc CMR 108-2   **Can. \$21.99 U.S.\$ 18.99**